TOP 10 VIENNA

MICHAEL LEIDIG
&
IRENE ZOECH

Left **Schloss Schönbrunn** Right **Josef Strauss statue, Stadtpark**

LONDON, NEW YORK,
MELBOURNE, MUNICH AND DELHI
www.dk.com

Produced by Sargasso Media Ltd, London
Printed and bound in China

First published in the UK in 2003 by Dorling Kindersley Limited, 80 Strand, London WC2R 0RL
A Penguin Random House Company
15 16 17 18 10 9 8 7 6 5 4 3 2 1

A CIP catalogue record is available from the British Library.

ISBN 978 0 24100 747 1

Within each Top 10 list in this book, no hierarchy of quality or popularity is implied. All 10 are, in the editor's opinion, of roughly equal merit.

MIX
Paper from responsible sources
FSC™ C018179

Contents

Vienna's Top 10

The information in this DK Eyewitness Top 10 Travel Guide is checked regularly.
Every effort has been made to ensure that this book is as up-to-date as possible at the time of going to press. Some details, however, such as telephone numbers, opening hours, prices, gallery hanging arrangements and travel information are liable to change. The publishers cannot accept responsibility for any consequences arising from the use of this book, nor for any material on third party websites, and cannot guarantee that any website address in this book will be a suitable source of travel information. We value the views and suggestions of our readers very highly. Please write to: Publisher, DK Eyewitness Travel Guides, Dorling Kindersley, 80 Strand, London WC2R 0RL, UK, or email: travelguides@dk.com.

Cover: Front – **AWL Images**: Neil Farrin main; **DK Images**: Peter Wilson/Courtesy of Schloss Schönbrunn, Vienna bl. Spine – **DK Images**: Peter Wilson b. Back – **DK Images**: Peter Wilson/Courtesy of Schloss Schönbrunn, Vienna tr; Peter Wilson tc, tl, tr.

Left **Stephansdom** Right **Spittelberg**

Around Town

Streetsmart

Left **Café Central, Central Vienna** Right **Baroque altar, Michaelerkirche**

Key to abbreviations
Adm *admission charge* **Free** *no admission charge* **Dis. access** *disabled access*

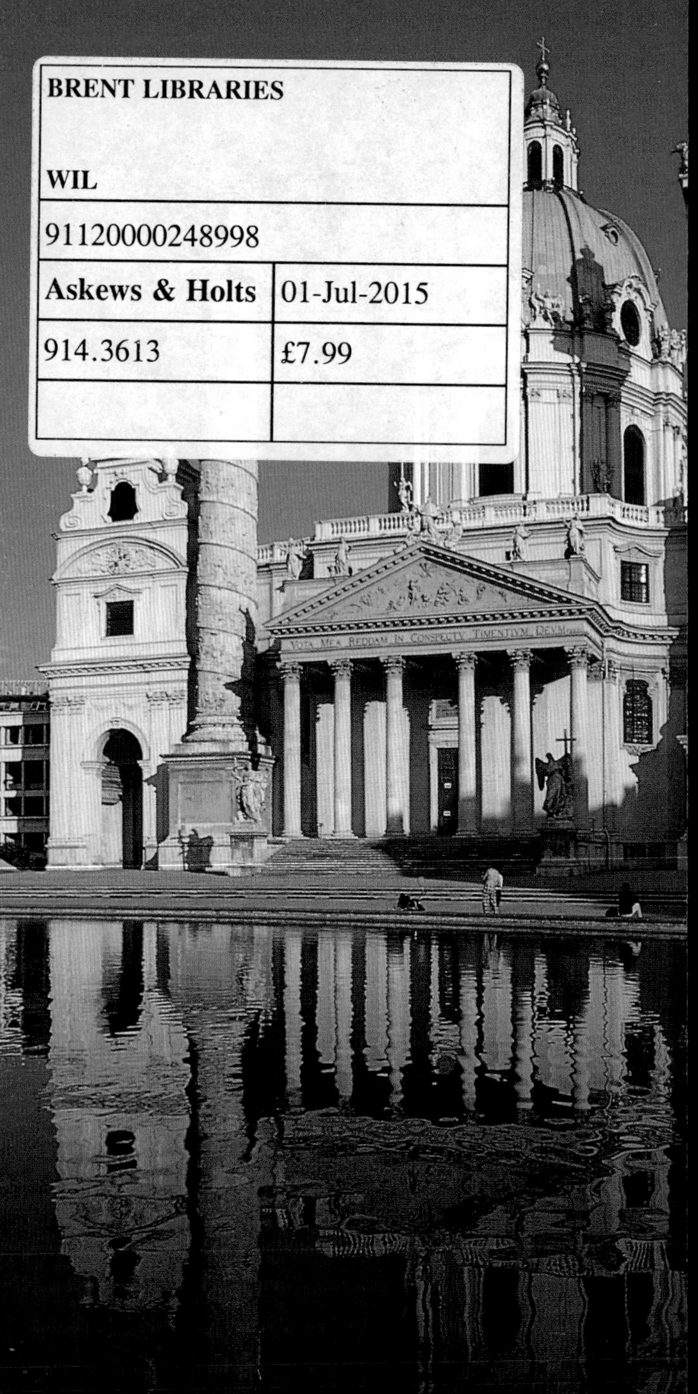
VOTA MEA REDDAM IN CONSPECTV TIMENTIVM DEVM

VIENNA'S TOP 10

VIENNA'S TOP 10

Top 10 Vienna's Highlights

Splendid edifices, magnificent palaces and imposing churches spanning the centuries all make Vienna a wonderful city to visit, oozing both charm and atmosphere. Although its imperial grandeur can still be felt, this city of music has more to offer than just its glorious past; contemporary architecture, a brimming cultural scene and vibrant nightlife add to its appeal. The following 10 sights are a must for any first-time visitor, but no matter how many times you return, you will always discover something new.

1 Stephansdom

The Gothic cathedral *(left)* is one of Vienna's most prominent landmarks, dominating the city centre. From its spire you can enjoy spectacular views over the rooftops *(see pp8–11)*.

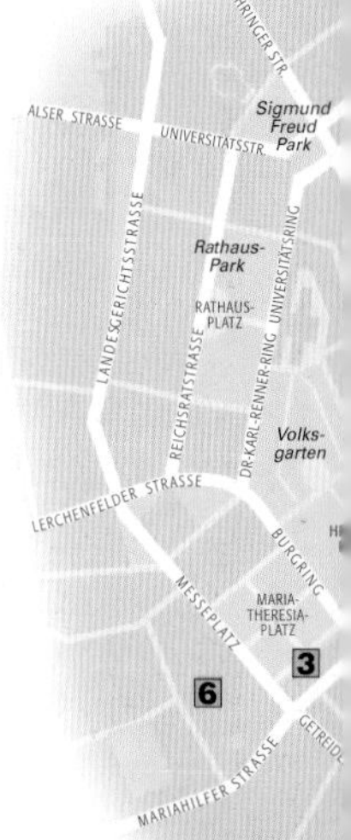

2 Hofburg Palace

The former imperial palace *(below)*, with its many wings and courtyards, has always been of historic importance. The interior reflects Austria's glorious past and is the setting for grand balls *(see pp12–17)*.

3 Kunsthistorisches Museum

This remarkable museum contains a stunning array of paintings, including one of the world's largest collections of Old Masters *(above) (see pp18–21)*.

4 The Belvedere

The former summer residence of the 17th-century war hero Prince Eugen is a splendid Baroque palace with vast French gardens, and is now home to the Austrian National Gallery *(left)*. It houses world-famous paintings by Austrian artists, including Gustav Klimt's Art Nouveau work *The Kiss* *(see pp22–5)*.

5 Karlskirche

This impressive Baroque church *(above)*, built in the early 18th century, has two distinguished columns on either side and a large dome overhead. It is a splendid sight dominating Karlsplatz *(see pp26–7)*.

6 Museumsquartier

The former imperial stables have been converted into a large museum complex *(left)*, exhibiting, among other things, collections of contemporary and modern art *(see pp28–9)*.

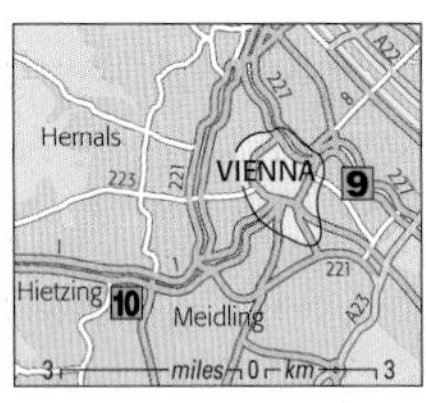

8 Secession Building

The simple white Secession building *(left)* is a magnificent Art Nouveau edifice that reflects the ideals of the Secessionist movement – purity and functionalism *(see pp32–3)*.

9 Hundertwasserhaus

Designed by Austrian artist Friedensreich Hundertwasser, this unconventional building *(above)* is characterized by uneven floors, rooftop gardens and unique windows *(see pp34–5)*.

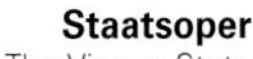

Staatsoper 7

The Vienna State Opera attracts music lovers from all over the world. Its entrance hall with a majestic staircase *(right)* is a fine introduction to an evening of classical music *(see pp30–31)*.

Schloss Schönbrunn 10

The former summer residence of the imperial Habsburg family remains today as a magnificent palace *(above)*, with splendid Baroque gardens and the world's oldest zoo. It attracts some 110,000 visitors a year *(see pp36–9)*.

TOP 10 Stephansdom

Located in the heart of the city, the Stephansdom is Vienna's most beloved landmark and Austria's finest Gothic edifice. The foundations of the original Romanesque church date back to 1147, but the earliest surviving features today are the 13th-century Giant's Door (Riesentor) *and the Heathen Towers* (Heidentürme) *on the west front. Various Habsburg rulers left their imprints by rebuilding the Gothic nave, the side chapels and the choir in the 14th and 15th centuries. The "Steffl", as the cathedral is lovingly called by the Viennese, suffered severe damage from World War II bombings, but its rebuilding was a symbol of hope as the country emerged from the ashes of the conflict.*

Giant's Door

Although you have to climb 343 steps to reach the visitor's platform in the South Tower, don't miss the stunning view across Vienna's rooftops. An alternative is the elevator up to the North Tower.

- *Stephansplatz*
- *Map N3*
- *01 515 52 3526*
- *www.stephanskirche.at*
- *Open 6am–10pm daily; guided tours 10:30am & 3pm Mon–Sat (also Jun–Sep: 7pm Sat), 3pm Sun & holidays; guided tours in English Apr–Oct: 3:45pm daily*
- *Dis. access (ground floor only)*
- *Adm: South Tower €4; North Tower €5*

Top 10 Features

1. West Front
2. Giant's Door
3. Tiled Roof
4. North Tower with Pummerin
5. Vaulting
6. High Altar
7. Organ
8. Catacombs
9. Windows
10. Pillars

1 West Front

The two Romanesque Heathen Towers flanking the Giant's Door *(right)*, and two Gothic side chapels with filigree stone rose windows, are a spectacular welcome to the cathedral.

2 Giant's Door

The main gate into the cathedral was named after a mammoth's bone that was found on the site during construction works in the 15th century. It is decorated with Romanesque sculptures depicting Christ on Judgment Day between two angels.

3 Tiled Roof

The impressive roof is covered with almost 250,000 colourful tiles laid out in the Habsburg coat of arms *(left)* – a double-headed eagle wearing the emperor's crown and the Golden Fleece. Originally constructed in 1490, the roof was restored after fire damage in World War II.

For more places of worship in Vienna **See pp48–9**

North Tower with Pummerin 4

The North Tower, topped with a cupola, is home to the "Pummerin" *(right)*. This bell, weighing nearly 20 tons, was cast from 100 cannonballs seized during the Turks' failed siege of Vienna in 1683.

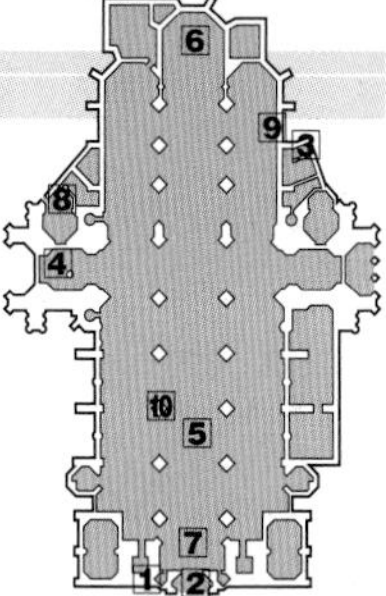

Plan of the Cathedral

6 High Altar

The beautiful Baroque high altar *(right)* was created by the brothers Tobias and Johann Pock in 1641. The painting in the centre of the marble altar depicts the stoning of the cathedral's patron saint, St Stephan.

7 Organ

The famous "Giant Organ", built in 1886, was destroyed during World War II. A large modern organ with 125 pipes *(below)* was installed in the west choir in 1960.

8 Catacombs

When Emperor Karl VI closed the cathedral cemetery in 1732, a catacomb system was constructed to bury the city's dead. By the end of the 18th century, about 11,000 people were laid to rest in the catacombs *(left)*. The centrepiece is the Duke's Crypt, which holds the remains of the Habsburgs.

5 Vaulting

The Gothic main nave is covered by an impressive ribbed vault supported by tall pillars.

9 Windows

The five colourful medieval windows behind the high altar tell biblical stories about the prophets and saints as well as the life and Passion of Jesus.

10 Pillars

The main nave is dominated by soaring pillars, lavishly decorated with 77 clay and stone statues dating back to the 15th century.

Cathedral Guide

Enter the cathedral through the Giant's Door at the west front. The Gothic pulpit is to your left, as is the elevator up to the top of the North Tower, just behind the organ base showing the self-portrait of cathedral builder Master Pilgram. The entrance to the catacombs is in the middle of the left side, past the Wiener Neustädter Altar. In the far right-hand corner is Emperor Friedrich III's raised tomb. *(See p10.)*

Left **Pulpit** Right **Master Pilgram**

Gothic Features in the Cathedral

1 Pulpit

The lavishly decorated pulpit was created by Anton Pilgram, one of the craftsmen working on the cathedral, in 1510. Lizards and toads, symbolizing evil, crawl up the balustrade, but they are fought off by a dog, the symbol of good.

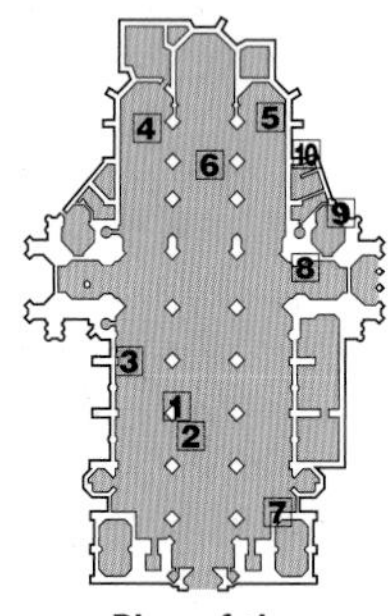

Plan of the Gothic Features

2 Fenstergucker

In this marvellous example of the Viennese late Gothic period, a sculpture of Master Pilgram himself leans out of an open window below the pulpit steps to inspect his work.

3 Master Pilgram

Another self-portrait of Master Pilgram that he included in his cathedral masterpiece can be seen at the base of the old organ. He is holding his tools – a pair of compasses in his right hand and a set square in his left hand.

Wiener Neustädter Altar

4 Wiener Neustädter Altar

The richly decorated altar with four wings shows 72 saints and scenes from the life of the Virgin Mary. Carved and painted in 1447, it was originally used as a shrine for relics.

5 Raised Tomb of Friedrich III

Friedrich III commissioned Niklas Gerhaert van Leyden to create for him a majestic raised tomb but it was only finished 20 years after the emperor's death. Little carved monks along the sarcophagus pray for his soul.

6 Baptismal Basin

Carved from red Salzburg marble, it took five years to finish this 14-sided basin. Its decorations show the seven holy sacraments, in the centre of which is Jesus's baptism.

7 Canopy with Pötscher Madonna

The 16th-century stone canopy shelters an icon of the Madonna from the Hungarian village of Pocs. In the 17th century the story spread that tears ran down Mary's cheeks and today people pray here for the sick to be healed.

8 Servants' Madonna

The graceful statue of the Madonna and Child is said to have miraculously helped acquit a maid who had been wrongly accused of stealing valuables from her master.

9 Cenotaph of Rudolf the Founder

Rudolf the Founder and his wife Katharina lie next to each other on their marble sarcophagus. The tomb was originally decorated with gold and precious jewels, and figures were placed in the little alcoves.

Gargoyles

10 Gargoyles

The gargoyles on the exterior roof of the cathedral are cast in the shape of dragons and other mythical animals in order to ward off evil.

Top 10 Events in the Cathedral

1. The first church on the site is consecrated (1147)
2. St Stephan gains the status of a diocese (1469)
3. Double wedding of Maximilian's grandchildren to the children of the Hungarian king (1515)
4. Wolfgang Amadeus Mozart weds Constanze Weber (1782)
5. Churchyard and cathedral are closed following a plague epidemic (1783)
6. Mozart's funeral (1791)
7. "October Revolution" rages in and around the Stephansdom (1848)
8. Emperor Franz Joseph's funeral (1916)
9. Fire destroys the cathedral's roof (1945)
10. Funeral of Zita, wife of the last Austrian emperor, Karl I (1989)

Johannes Capistranus and the Turkish Siege

On the northeastern exterior wall of the cathedral is an elaborate Baroque pulpit cast in honour of the Franciscan saint, Johannes Capistranus (1385–1456). Born in Capestrano, Italy, Johannes gave up the legal life in which he had trained after having a dream in which the vision of St Francis urged him to join the Franciscan Order. He became a priest in 1425 and soon gained a huge following, with adoring crowds flocking to hear him preach against heresy all over Italy. But it was for his peacemaking skills that he was most highly regarded. After successful missions in Italy and France, he was sent to Austria in 1451 to preach against the Turkish invasion, and he led the Christian army to victory against the Turks in the battle of Belgrade in 1456. Johannes was canonized in 1724; later that century the Austrians erected the pulpit in gratitude, depicting the saint victoriously trampling a defeated Turkish invader.

Pulpit of Johannes Capistranus

Top 10 Hofburg Palace

The Hofburg, Vienna's former Imperial Palace, is a lavish complex of buildings spread over a considerable area within the city centre. Once home to emperors, the medieval castle was enlarged gradually up until 1918, and as the power of the Habsburgs grew, successive emperors added buildings in contemporary styles – the New Palace (Neue Burg) *is the most recent and spectacular section. Today the Hofburg houses the offices of the Austrian president, an international convention centre, the Winter Riding School where the elegant white Lipizzaner stallions of the Spanish Riding School perform* (see pp16–17), *various official and private apartments, and several museums and state rooms which are open to the public.*

Imperial Apartments

Every Sunday the Vienna Boys' Choir sings mass at 9:15am in the Imperial Chapel. Book tickets in advance.

- *Innerer Burghof/ Kaisertor*
- *Map L4*
- *01 533 75 70*
- *www.hofburg-wien.at*
- *Open Sep–Jun: 9am–5:30pm daily; Jul & Aug: 9am–6pm daily*
- *Dis. access*
- *Adm €11.50*

Top 10 Features

1. Imperial Apartments
2. Swiss Gate
3. Imperial Silver Collection
4. Secular and Ecclesiastical Treasuries
5. Imperial Chapel
6. National Library
7. Heroes' Square
8. Museums
9. Burggarten and Volksgarten
10. Michaeler Gate

1 Imperial Apartments

The private apartments *(Kaiserappartements)* in the Amalia Wing are preserved as they were in the day of Emperor Franz Joseph and his wife Elisabeth *(see p15)*. Six rooms are dedicated to her as the Sisi Museum.

2 Swiss Gate

The name of this Renaissance gate *(below)* refers to the Swiss guards employed by Empress Maria Theresa in the 18th century.

3 Imperial Silver Collection

This collection of elaborate table decorations, serving bowls and silverware is proof of the splendour that marked meals at the imperial court.

4 Secular and Ecclesiastical Treasuries

Magnificent artifacts are on display here, such as lavish monstrances. Sixteen rooms are dedicated to the gems and relics of both the Austrian and the Holy Roman Empires.

The Hofburg complex has 18 wings, 54 staircases and some 2,600 rooms.

5 Imperial Chapel

Although the original Gothic interior with carved statuary *(left)* was altered by Maria Theresa, the chapel *(Burgkapelle)* remains one of the oldest parts of the palace. The atmosphere of former times can still be felt, where once composers such as Mozart gave musical performances.

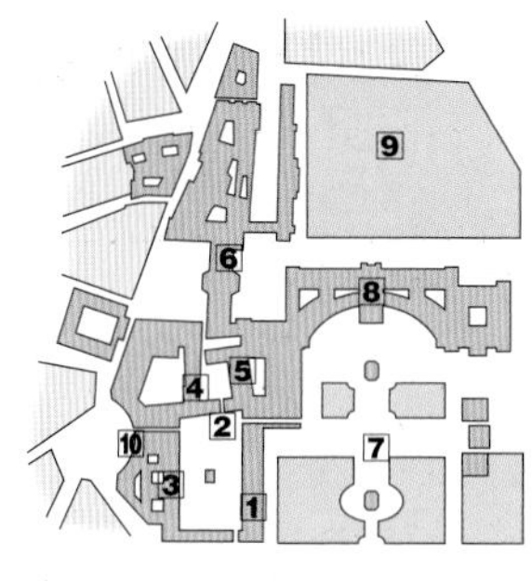

Plan of the Hofburg Palace

6 National Library

The Baroque library *(below)* was constructed by Josef Emanuel Fischer von Erlach from 1723 to 1726. It is considered to be among the world's finest, with invaluable historic manuscripts in walnut-wood bookcases.

7 Heroes' Square

Equestrian statues of Prince Eugen of Savoy and Archduke Charles dominate the large Heroes' Square *(Heldenplatz)*, which was formerly a parade ground.

8 Museums

The semi-circular Neue Burg, with its vast colonnaded façade, is home to a collection of musical instruments as well as an assemblage of arms and armour. Also housed here is the Weltmuseum Wien ethnological museum *(see p14)*.

9 Burggarten and Volksgarten

Both parks owe their origins to the Napoleonic troops who blew up parts of the palace in 1809 to make way for greenery.

10 Michaeler Gate

The majestic semicircular Michaeler Gate is the main entrance into the complex, and its imposing dome with golden decorations *(above)* looms over Michaelerplatz.

Building the Palace

Every emperor up to 1918 left his imprint on the building. The Stallburg was built in the Renaissance under Maximilian II, while Amalienburg, built for Maximilian's son Rudolf, was completed in 1605. The oldest surviving part is the Schweizertrakt, with the Imperial Chapel and the Swiss Gate (1552–3).

In 1938, on Heroes' Square, the masses cheered Adolf Hitler when he announced the incorporation of Austria into the Third Reich.

Left **Austrian Sceptre and Orb** Right **The Golden Fleece**

Top 10 Artistic Treasures in the Palace

1 Silverware and Porcelain
The *Silberkammer* displays the silverware and Augarten porcelain used for imperial banquets.

2 Crown of the Holy Roman Empire
Among the palace's collection of secular and ecclesiastical objects is this gold crown, crafted around AD 962 and decorated with *cloisonné* enamel and gemstones.

3 Austrian Sceptre and Orb
The enthroning of a new Habsburg ruler was accompanied by a ceremony of homage, during which the sovereign carried the sceptre and orb.

4 Cradle of the King of Rome
This cradle was given by Maria Louisa to her son, the King of Rome. It is adorned with precious materials such as gold, silver and mother-of-pearl, while a goddess of victory crowns the child with a diadem of stars and a laurel wreath.

5 The Golden Fleece
This splendid chain-mail armour, made in 1517, consists of a neck chain and a closed collar of double-walled plates.

6 Captain Cook Artifacts
Among the exhibits in the Weltmuseum Wien are artifacts acquired by Captain James Cook on his voyages, including masks from North America.

7 Historic Globes
This collection unites more than 300 historic globes and astrological instruments, including two globes made by Vincenzo Coronelli for Emperor Leopold I.

8 National Library Frescoes
Daniel Gran painted these frescoes in 1730 to honour Emperor Karl VI. The statue in the middle of the room represents the emperor as the centre of the universe, holding a balance between war and peace.

9 Aztec Feather Headpiece
Crafted in the 16th century with more than 450 shiny green-tail Quetzal feathers, this headpiece is one of only eight of its kind surviving worldwide.

10 Portrait of Empress Elisabeth
Franz Xavier Winterhalter painted this famous portrait in 1865. It hangs in one of the rooms of the Sisi Museum *(see p12)*.

Cradle of the King of Rome

Top 10 Events in the Hofburg Palace

1. A fort is built on the site of today's Hofburg (1275)
2. Alte Burg wing is built under Ferdinand I (1547–52)
3. Fischer von Erlach starts building the Winter Riding School (1729)
4. Carousels with the Lipizzaner horses staged in the Winter Riding School (1740–80)
5. Mozart performs regularly in the Burgkapelle between 1781 and 1791
6. Vienna Congress is held (1815)
7. Michaeler wing is built (1889–93)
8. World War I prevents the construction of the second wing (1918)
9. Hitler proclaims the Austrian annexation to the Third Reich from the balcony of Neue Burg (1938)
10. Fire destroys the ballroom in the Redoute wing (1992)

The Reforming Emperor

After many years of political upheaval *(see p40)*, Emperor Franz Joseph was a breath of fresh air to Viennese life. With the construction of the elegant Ringstrasse, he ushered in a new age of grandeur and the city became a magnet for artists, writers, composers and other creative people.

Franz Joseph and Sisi

Born in 1830, Franz Joseph was crowned Emperor of Austria in 1848, aged 18. He met his wife Princess Elisabeth of Bavaria, lovingly known to Austrians as "Sisi", in 1853 and they married shortly after. The empress was adored by Austrians, then as now, for her extraordinary beauty, dignity and elegance in state matters – many believed Franz Joseph's social successes were the result of Sisi's influence, and they considered her their "real" sovereign. The lives of the emperor and empress were not without trials and sorrows, however. Franz Joseph lost major wars to France (1848) and Prussia (1866), despite being crowned King of Hungary in 1867. They also suffered many personal tragedies – the emperor's brother, Maximilian, was executed in Mexico and his only son, Crown Prince Rudolf, committed suicide in 1889, after which Sisi dressed only in black. Austria, too, fell into mourning in 1898 when their beloved empress was assassinated in Geneva. Franz Joseph was to rule Austria until his death in 1916.

Empress Elisabeth

Left, Centre & Right **Lipizzaner horse displays**

Spanish Riding School Features

1 Lipizzaner Horses

The elegant white Lipizzaner stallions are bred at the national stud farm at Piber. The foals are born dark-skinned or black and acquire their trademark white coat between the ages of four and ten years.

2 Training

The horses move from the stud farm to the Spanish Riding School when they are about four years old and are then trained for eight years, or sometimes longer, until they are skilled enough to perform.

3 Horses' Steps

The steps follow the rigid patterns of the "high art" of riding which was established during the Renaissance period. It is based on horseback battle manoeuvres. The most difficult part of the performance is the school quadrille, which involves a precise and exact framework of choreography.

4 Riders

Just like the horses, the riders have to go through an extensive training period for classical dressage and other riding techniques. The riders traditionally wear white jodhpurs and a double-breasted coffee-brown coat with brass buttons.

Portrait of Karl VI

5 Stables

The Renaissance building in the Stallburg section of the Hofburg has a three-storey gallery, built during the reign of Emperor Maximilian.

6 Winter Riding School

Since 1735 the Spanish Riding School has been located in the Winter Riding School building, designed by Fischer von Erlach in Baroque style.

7 Interior

The horses perform their balet in the 56-m- (180-ft-) long hall. The gallery is supported by 46 Corinthian columns.

8 Emperor's Box

The box at the narrow side of the hall was reserved for the emperor and his family.

9 Portrait of Karl VI

A portrait of Karl VI riding on a white stallion hangs in the royal box. Riders entering the hall pay respect to the founder of the school by raising their bicorn hats to the painting.

10 Summer Riding School

In summer, performances and training at the Spanish Riding School are carried out in a courtyard adjoining the Winter Riding School.

Top 10 Pieces of Tackle and Equipment

1. Bicorn hats
2. Jackets
3. Buckskin jodhpurs
4. High boots
5. Spurs
6. Saddle
7. Pale leather gloves
8. Curb reins
9. Gala uniform
10. Summer uniform

The History of the Lipizzaner Horses

Spanish horses were first brought to Austria from Spain by Emperor Maximilian II in 1562, and the first documented evidence of them being housed in the Hofburg's Spanish Riding School (Spanische Reitschule) *dates back to 1572. In 1580 the horses were given the name Lipizzaner after a stud farm in Trieste and around that time the first riding hall was built at the present location in Josefplatz. The school as we know it today was formed in the 19th century and played host to splendid equestrian events for high-standing international audiences in which the horses performed in graceful circular formations. But its entertaining days ended in 1894, when it took on a more militant role to train riders and horses in classical disciplines. In 1918, after World War I, the school was taken over by the newly formed Austrian Republic and for the first time opened its doors to the general public.*

Imperial Celebrations

The Spanish Riding School was used to celebrate Habsburg victories, such as the defeat of the French army at Prague in 1743 *(below)*. Crown Prince Rudolf *(left)* was among many imperial family members to join in on equestrian activities.

Kunsthistorisches Museum

Built in the style of the Italian Renaissance by architects Karl von Hasenauer and Gottfried Semper, the impressive Kunsthistorisches Museum (Museum of Fine Arts) was opened in 1891. Its completion meant that, for the first time, most of the imperial collection of art was housed under one roof. The magnificent architecture creates a fitting setting for the artistic treasures assembled by the Habsburgs, who were enthusiastic patrons and collectors for centuries. The collections of the museum, particularly the Old Masters, are among the most important and spectacular in the world.

Façade

Don't miss the spectacular view of the white marble floor with black patterns from the café on the first floor.

- *Maria-Theresien-Platz*
- *Map K5*
- *01 525 24 0*
- *www.khm.at*
- *Open 10am–6pm Tue–Sun (until 9pm Thu)*
- *Dis. access (entrance at Burgring 5)*
- *Adm €14, concessions €11 (free entry for under 19s)*

Top 10 Works of Art

1. The Fur
2. Large Self-Portrait
3. Peasant Wedding
4. Madonna of the Cherries
5. Virgin and Child with a Pear
6. Summer
7. Maria Theresa's Breakfast Service
8. Blue Hippo
9. Stela of Ha-hat, Thebes
10. St Gregory with the Scribes

1 The Fur

This painting *(right)* is the most intimate portrait of Peter Paul Rubens' wife (1638), whom he married late in life and whose features he often incorporated into his works. In a naturally graceful pose, the young woman evokes Venus, the classical goddess of love.

2 Large Self-Portrait

The Dutch master Rembrandt painted this canvas in 1652, depicting everything around him in dark colours, with his face the only area of light.

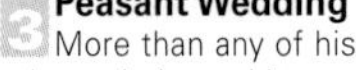

3 Peasant Wedding

More than any of his other paintings, this one *(left)* contributed to Pieter Brueghel the Elder's fame as a portrayer of peasant life. He painted the picture on wood in 1568. The viewer feels right in the middle of a rustic wedding.

For more museums and art galleries in Vienna **See pp42–5**

Key

Ground floor

First floor

Entrance

4 Madonna of the Cherries

A number of paintings by Titian can be found in the Italian Collection. In this one (1518), the Madonna's dress is painted in the red-brown colours for which the artist is famous.

5 Virgin and Child with a Pear

German artist Albrecht Dürer painted many Madonna pictures, but this one *(below)* is among the best known, showing the Virgin Mary bending over a child holding a pear core.

6 Summer

From 1562 Giuseppe Arcimboldo served as portrait artist and organizer of festivities at the court of Rudolf II. The Italian painter became famous for his heads composed of various fruits and vegetables which served as allegorical representations *(left)*.

7 Maria Theresa's Breakfast Service

Crafted in Vienna around 1750, this pure gold set belonged to the empress and consists of about 70 pieces. Some items, such as a mirror and a basin, are part of a washing set.

8 Blue Hippo

Figurines of hippos are often found in Middle Kingdom tombs (c.2000 BC) of Ancient Egypt, and this example has images of its habitat painted on its body. Hunting hippos was once a royal privilege granted to subjects.

9 Stela of Ha-hat, Thebes

The stela (stone slab), which is more than 2,500 years old, is lavishly painted in gold, red and blue and depicts Osiris among other Egyptian gods, who are praised in the inscriptions. The stela was discovered inside a tomb in Thebes.

10 St Gregory with the Scribes

This late 9th-century ivory carving from Germany *(left)* shows St Gregory working with three scribes.

Museum Guide

The main entrance is on Maria-Theresien-Platz – the square between the Natural History Museum and Museum of Fine Arts. As you enter, collect a map to guide you through the exhibition. On the ground floor are the Egyptian Collection and the Greek and Roman Antiquities to your right, while the left wing hosts the magnificent Kunstkammer (Chamber of Art and Wonders). The staircase takes you to the first floor, where the Picture Gallery with the most famous paintings is located. The Coin Cabinet is on the second floor.

Left **Canaletto, Italian Collection** Right **16th-century coin, Coin Cabinet**

Top 10 Kunsthistorisches Collections

1 Italian Collection

Most of the 15th- to 18th-century Italian paintings were collected by Archduke Leopold Wilhelm, who founded the collection in the 17th century. They are mainly from the Venetian Renaissance with major works by Titian, Veronese, Canaletto and Tintoretto.

2 Dutch Collection

The Dutch section (15th to 17th century) has a comprehensive collection of works by Pieter Brueghel the Elder, containing about a third of all his surviving pictures. Pictures by Rembrandt, Pieter de Hooch and Gerard ter Borch are also on display.

Portrait of Gonella, Court Jester at the Court of Ferrara, artist unknown, Dutch Collection

3 Flemish Collection

Several works from 17th-century Flanders made their way into the museum because of Habsburg family ties to this part of Europe. The highlights of the collection are works by Rubens and Jan van Eyck.

4 German Collection

The German collection has a great number of 16th-century paintings. Among them are works by Albrecht Dürer, Lucas Cranach the Elder and Hans Holbein the Younger.

5 Spanish and French Collection

Thanks to Habsburg family ties, portraits of the Spanish royal family made their way into the collection. Diego Velázquez's portraits of the Infanta Margarita Teresa (Philip IV's daughter) are on display.

6 Egyptian Collection

This section has a remarkably extensive stock of monuments of the "Old Kingdom". The collection emerged in the 19th and 20th centuries, developed by purchases, donations and new acquisitions from excavations.

7 Greek and Roman Antiquities

The collection originating from the former estate of the Habsburgs covers a period of history extending from Cypriot

Adam and Eve in the Garden of Eden, Lucas Cranach the Elder, German Collection

Bronze Age pottery from the 3rd century BC to Slavic finds from around the beginning of the 1st century AD. It is also internationally renowned as the home of the unique cameos and archaeological treasures dating from the Great Migration and the Early Middle Ages.

8 Kunstkammer (Chamber of Art and Wonders)

This area consists largely of works from former Habsburg collections in various residences. The richest part of the Kunstkammer Collection is the immense treasure of Emperor Rudolf II which was saved from the turmoil of wars. Among the highlights are the famous *Saliera* (salt cellar) by Benvenuto Cellini and Maria Theresa's breakfast service, as well as bronze, ivory and wood sculptures, exotic objects and curiosities.

Blue hippo, Egyptian Collection

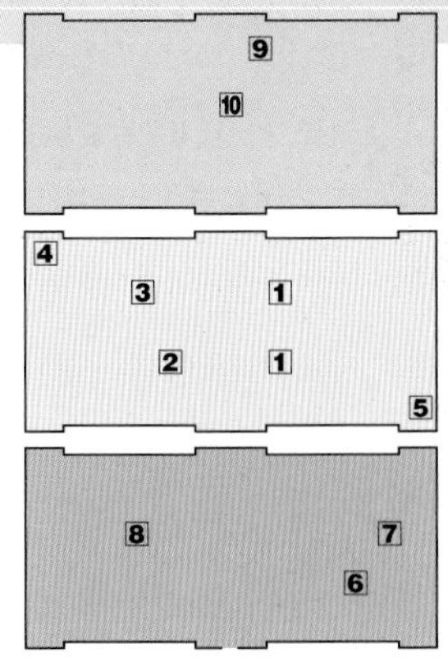

Key to the Collections

- Ground floor
- First floor
- Second floor

9 Coin Cabinet

More than 700,000 coins, medals and banknotes from three millennia are on display in the numismatic collection.

10 The Vermeyen Cartoons

These large sketches, or "cartoons", depict scenes from Emperor Charles V's Tunis campaign of 1535. They were produced by court painter Jan Cornelisz Vermeyen (who accompanied the Emperor on the campaign), and used by Willem de Pannemaker as models for 12 tapestries which now hang in Madrid.

TOP 10 The Belvedere

Prince Eugen of Savoy, the most celebrated of the Habsburg generals due to his defeat of the Turks in 1683, commissioned the two Belvedere palaces (Upper and Lower) with the money he received as a reward for his victories during the Spanish Succession. The payment allowed him to carry out one of the most ambitious building projects ever undertaken by a private individual. The palaces were built by Lukas von Hildebrandt in 1714–23 as a summer residence for the prince and are a shining example of Baroque style.

Upper Belvedere façade

For hearty Austrian food as well as specially brewed beer, try Salm Bräu, on Rennweg, next to the Belvedere Palace *(see p120)*.

Visit the Palace Stables to see some 150 objects of sacred medieval art.

- *Upper Belvedere: Prinz-Eugen-Strasse 27; Map G6*
- *Lower Belvedere: Rennweg 6; Map F5*
- *01 796 57 0*
- *www.belvedere.at*
- *Upper Belvedere open 10am–6pm daily; Lower Belvedere and Orangery open 10am–6pm daily (to 9pm Wed); Palace Stables open 10am–noon daily (groups by prior arrangement)* • *Dis. access*
- *Adm Upper Belvedere €12.50; Lower Belvedere €11; combined ticket €19 (includes Orangery and Palace Stables)*

Top 10 Features

1. Orangery
2. Lower Belvedere
3. Marble Gallery
4. Mirror Cabinet
5. French Gardens
6. Garden Statues
7. Sala Terrena
8. Stairways
9. Marble Hall
10. Upper Belvedere Façade

1 Orangery

Once home to the Museum of Austrian Medival Art, the Orangery is now a temporary exhibition hall. It has a corridor which offers a breathtaking view onto the Privy Garden and the Upper Belvedere.

2 Lower Belvedere

Formerly the Museum of Austrian Baroque Art, this is now used for temporary exhibitions only *(above)*. It includes the former living quarters and staterooms.

3 Marble Gallery

This grandiose room contains works by Georg Raphael Donner and the original lead figures of the Providentia Fountain, now on Hoher Markt.

4 Mirror Cabinet

A statue of Prince Eugen of Savoy stands in this Lower Belvedere room *(above)*. The walls are entirely covered by huge gilt-framed mirrors.

5 French Gardens

The French-style gardens link the palaces. The three levels each convey classical allusions: the lower part represents the Four Elements; the centre, Parnassus; and the upper section, Olympus.

6 Garden Statues

Among the numerous statues *(above)*, the Eight Muses and the Sphinxes are the most outstanding.

7 Sala Terrena

Its manifold architectural forms and sculptures make this Upper Belvedere hall one of the finest Baroque entrances. Four Herculean figures sculpted by Lorenzo Mattielli support the ceiling vault.

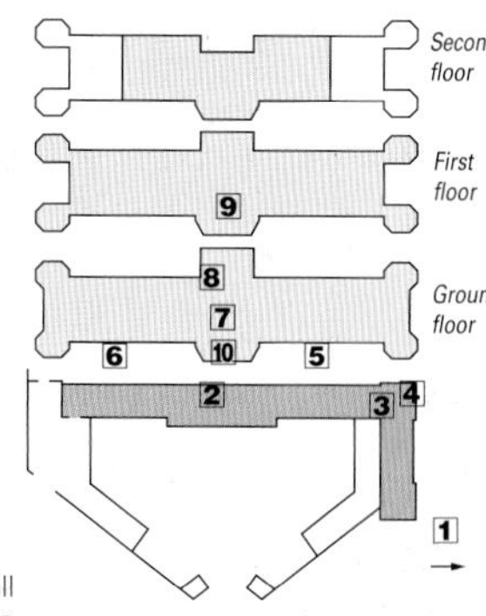

Key to the Belvedere

	Upper Belvedere
	Lower Belvedere

10 Upper Belvedere Façade

The Upper Belvedere's elaborate façade dominates the sweeping entrance. Its domed copper roofs resemble the shape of Turkish tents as a symbolic reflection of Prince Eugen's victory.

Signing the State Treaty

In 1955 the Upper Belvedere was the scene of rejoicing when the State Treaty was signed by the four powers that had occupied Austria since the end of World War II. In the Marble Hall John Foster Dulles (US), Harold Macmillan (UK), Vyacheslav Molotov (USSR) and Antoine Pinay (France) put their signatures to the document granting sovereignty to the country. The State Treaty was then displayed from the balcony to cheering crowds below.

8 Stairways

In the centre of the magnificent Upper Belvedere entrance hall are the Baroque stairways *(left)*, which lead to the ceremonial room.

9 Marble Hall

The central room of the Upper Belvedere was used for receptions and state occasions. The Austrian State Treaty was signed here in 1955.

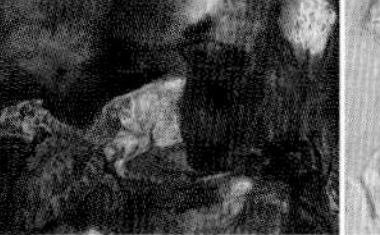

Left **Death and the Maiden** Centre **Still Life with Dead Lamb** Right **The Chef**

Top 10 Artworks in the Belvedere

1 The Kiss

Gustav Klimt's most celebrated work (1909) reflects the impression made on the artist by the mosaics of Italy.

2 Death and the Maiden

A man and a woman are clutching each other on a sheet spread over uneven terrain (1915). Artist Egon Schiele painted his own features on the man.

3 Still Life with Dead Lamb

This still life (1910) is one of the most important works by Oskar Kokoschka, seen as a metaphor of a world that has lost its way.

4 Laughing Self-Portrait

Painted the same year that the artist committed suicide (1908), Richard Gerstl tries a last attempt at defiant self-definition.

Laughing Self-Portrait

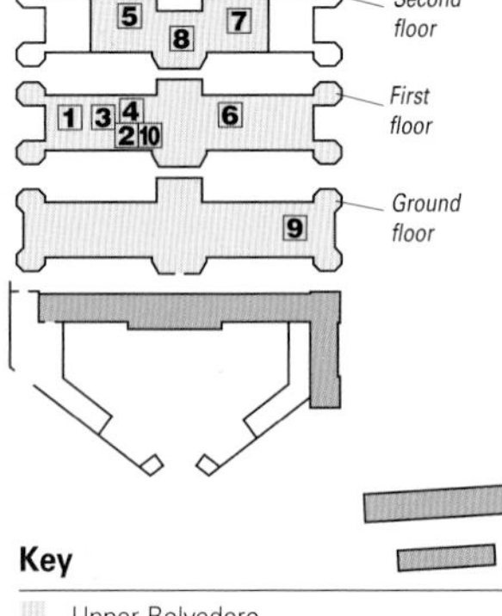

Key

Upper Belvedere

Lower Belvedere

5 Cliff Landscape in the Elb Sandstone Mountains

The North German romanticist Caspar David Friedrich sought in his paintings to relate man to the infinity of creation, showing his own transience. In describing natural phenomena, a transcendental element is always present. Thus his art, as seen in this landscape, was highly symbolistic (1822–3).

6 Character Heads

Franz Xavier Messerschmidt was one of the most eccentric artists of the 18th century. The series entitled "Character Heads" (1770–83) involves busts in which facial expressions and different moods are conveyed to the extreme. Among the highlights is the amusing "Intentional Jester".

7 Napoleon at the Saint Bernard Pass

Jacques-Louis David's idealized rendering of Napoleon (1803) depicts him crossing the Alps into Italy in 1801 on a white stallion. In fact, Bonaparte made this journey on a mule.

8 The Chef

Claude Monet painted only a few portraits. Staying at a small hotel on the Normandy coast, he painted its owner, the renowned cook Paul Antoine Graff (1882). Monet's depiction of the 60-year-old is economical and captures a typical facial expression with skilful spontaneity.

9 Znaimer Altarpiece

The carved inner sides of this triptych (c.1427) show the events of Good Friday as recorded in the Gospel According to St Matthew, supplemented by scenes taken from the Apocrypha.

10 Farmhouse in Upper Austria

Although Klimt is largely known for his figural-symbolistic pictures, landscape painting also played an important part in his work. From 1900 Klimt spent nearly all his summers in the Salzkammergut, painting scenes such as this one (1911).

Top 10 Austrian 19th- and 20th-Century Artists

1. Gustav Klimt (1862–1918)
2. Kolo Moser (1868–1918)
3. Richard Gerstl (1883–1908)
4. Oskar Kokoschka (1886–1980)
5. Egon Schiele (1890–1918)
6. Maria Lassnig (1919–2014)
7. Friedensreich Hundertwasser (1928–2000)
8. Hermann Nitsch (b.1938)
9. Christian Ludwig Attersee (b.1940)
10. Arnulf Rainer (b.1948)

The Secession Movement

The cultural climate of Vienna around 1900 owed a great deal to Gustav Klimt. In 1897 he founded the "Association of Austrian Artists – the Secession", a movement that wanted to break free from tradition. Its main style was bright colours, flowing human forms and stylized plants. It was a time of awakening in the art movement and it blessed Vienna with a host of important artists. In the architectural field, for example, Otto Wagner led the way to reform, followed by Adolf Loos. The Secession's idea of holistic art, modelling all aspects of life in one cast, caught on and in 1903 led to the founding of the Vienna Workshop. Artists such as Koloman Moser and Bernhard Löffler were behind most of its creations. The painters Oskar Kokoschka, Richard Gerstl and Egon Schiele soon followed and avidly continued the work of the Secession.

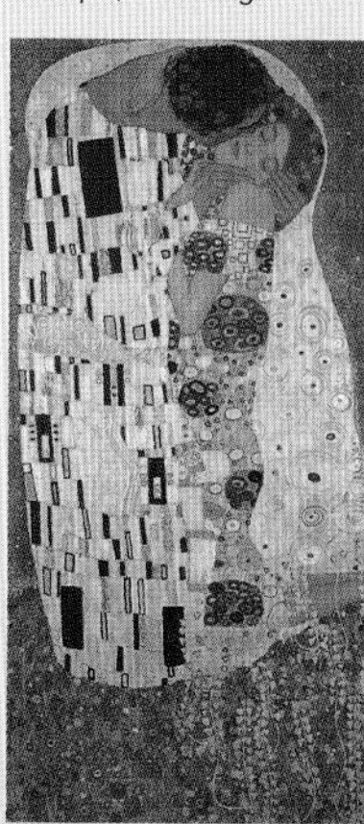

Klimt's The Kiss
Having visited Ravenna and Venice in Italy, Klimt was overawed by the mosaic work and adapted the idea into this glittering, erotic work.

Top 10 Karlskirche

This striking church was built between 1715 and 1737 to honour Karl Borromeo, the patron saint of the fight against the plague. Its aim was to thank God for delivering Vienna from the plague epidemic in 1713 that claimed more than 8,000 lives. Emperor Karl VI held a competition among architects to design the church, which was won by Johann Fischer von Erlach. The Baroque masterpiece has a dome and portico borrowed from Classical architecture, while there are Oriental echoes in the minaret-like columns.

Top of one of the gatehouses

Take the elevator to the top of the dome to get a close look at the frescoes and enjoy amazing views over the rooftops of Vienna.

- *Karlsplatz*
- *Map F4*
- *01 505 62 94*
- *www.karlskirche.at*
- *Open 9am–6pm Mon–Sat; noon–5:45pm Sun & holidays*
- *Dis. access*
- *Adm €8 (inc. elevator)*

Top 10 Features

1. Entrance
2. Columns
3. Karl Borromeo Statue
4. Pediment Reliefs
5. Angels
6. Cupola with Frescoes
7. High Altar
8. Pulpit
9. Altar Paintings
10. Pond with Henry Moore Sculpture

1 Entrance

The church façade is winged by two gatehouses that are reminiscent of Chinese pavilions and lead into the side entrances. At the centre of the façade is the stairway, above which is a pediment supported by six pillars.

2 Columns

Inspired by the ancient Roman column of Trajan, these columns are decorated with scenes of the life of St Karl Borromeo *(above)*. The left column shows the quality of steadfastness and the right shows courage.

3 Karl Borromeo Statue

Lorenzo Mattielli designed a statue of the patron saint of the fight against the plague. It has pride of place on the church's pediment *(below)*.

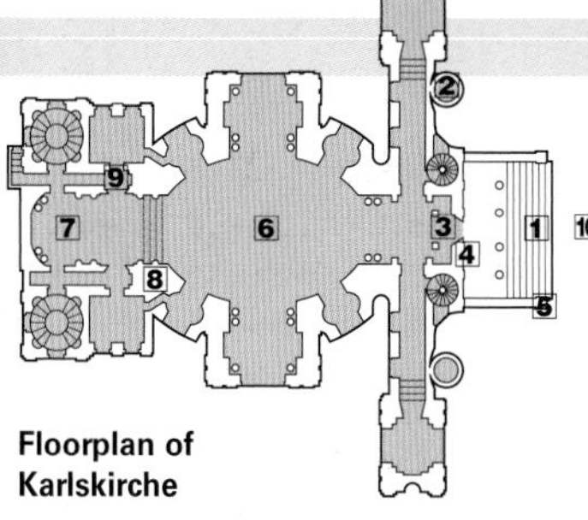

Floorplan of Karlskirche

4 Pediment Reliefs

The pediment *(above)* resembles the covering of a Greek temple and its reliefs, designed by Giovanni Stanetti, show the suffering of the Viennese during the 1713 plague.

5 Angels

Two angels guard the stairway as a sign of Catholic belief. The angel on the left represents the Old Testament; the other, the New Testament.

6 Cupola with Frescoes

Johann Michael Rottmayr's fresco on the dome *(right)* depicts the Virgin Mary begging the Holy Trinity to deliver the population from the plague.

7 High Altar

The typical Baroque-style high altar *(left)* was probably designed by Fischer von Erlach himself. It features a stucco relief by Albert Camesina showing St Karl Borromeo being taken into heaven on a cloud laden with angels and cherubs.

8 Pulpit

The church's richly gilded pulpit *(right)* is surmounted by two cherubs on the canopy and is decorated with *rocailles* (scrolls) and garlands of flowers.

9 Altar Paintings

The side altars are decorated with several paintings, but the most remarkable are those by master artist Daniel Gran. His famous paintings *The Healing of a Gout Victim, Jesus and the Roman Captain* and *Saint Elisabeth of Hungary* can be found in the church.

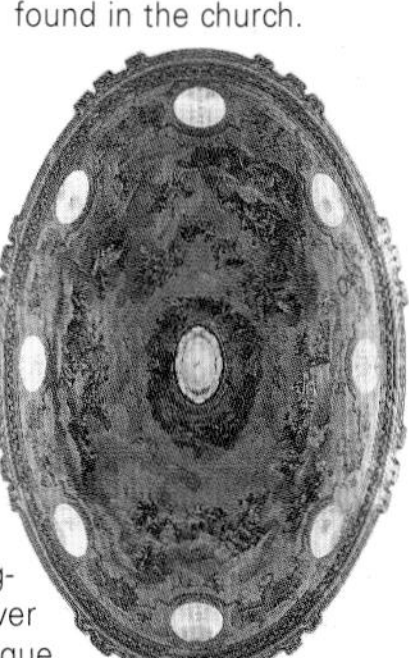

10 Pond with Henry Moore Sculpture

The setting of the Karlskirche is as impressive as its interior. In front of the church is a stone-paved pond with a modern sculpture by Henry Moore in the centre, deliberately intended to contrast with the Baroque style of the church.

Johann Fischer von Erlach

Many of Vienna's finest buildings were designed by Fischer von Erlach (1656–1723). The Graz-born architect studied in Rome, and then moved to Vienna, where he became the court architect and a leading exponent of the Baroque style. He designed many churches and palaces, notably the Karlskirche and the university church at Salzburg. Moreover, he sketched the plans for Schönbrunn palace *(see pp36–9)*. After his death, the Karlskirche was completed by his son.

TOP 10 Museumsquartier

The Baroque building that was once home to the emperors' horses is today one of the world's largest museum complexes. Commissioned by Karl VI in 1713 and completed by Johann Fischer von Erlach in 1725, the stables were transformed into an exhibition ground in 1918. In the 1990s the historic complex was turned into a huge cultural centre that opened in 2001. Today it includes the Museum of Modern Art Ludwig Foundation (MUMOK), the Kunsthalle and theatres. At the heart of the city, the Museumsquartier is one of Vienna's hot spots, with young people flocking to the trendy cafés and tranquil green areas.

Museum of Modern Art façade

If you fancy a cup of coffee or a snack, head for the pretty Oriental-style café in the Architectural Centre Vienna.

Take note of the opening times of the various museums in the complex, as all of them are different.

- *Museumsplatz 1*
- *Map J5*
- *01 523 58 81*
- *www.mqw.at*
- *Museum of Modern Art: Open 2–7pm Mon, 10am–7pm Tue–Sun (until 9pm Thu); Dis. access; Adm €10 (free entry for under 19s)*
- *Leopold Museum: Open 10am–6pm Mon, Wed, Fri–Sun; 10am–9pm Thu; Dis. access; Adm €12*
- *Architectural Centre Vienna: Open 10am–7pm daily; Adm €7*

Top 10 Features

1. Exterior
2. Fischer von Erlach Wing
3. Stables
4. Winter Riding Hall
5. Courtyards
6. Staircases
7. Leopold Museum
8. Museum of Modern Art
9. Architectural Centre Vienna
10. Zoom Kindermuseum

1 Exterior

The façade of the Museumsquartier is a majestic sight thanks to the complex's vast size. During the night rows of rod-shaped lamps bathe the edifice in light.

2 Fischer von Erlach Wing

The Baroque Fischer von Erlach Wing *(centre)*, constructed from 1713 to 1725, is painted in a shade of ochre. The imposing structure clearly dominates the whole complex, stretching out along the Ringstrasse, which encircles the city centre.

3 Stables

The barrel-vaulted rooms inside the Fischer von Erlach Wing once contained the stables for 600 horses. Today the rooms *(right)* house a number of cultural facilities known as Quartier 21.

4 Winter Riding Hall

The hall where the horses once had their winter training today hosts two stages. The theatre on the upper floor has a vaulted ceiling and is connected to the smaller theatre on the ground floor by two stairways.

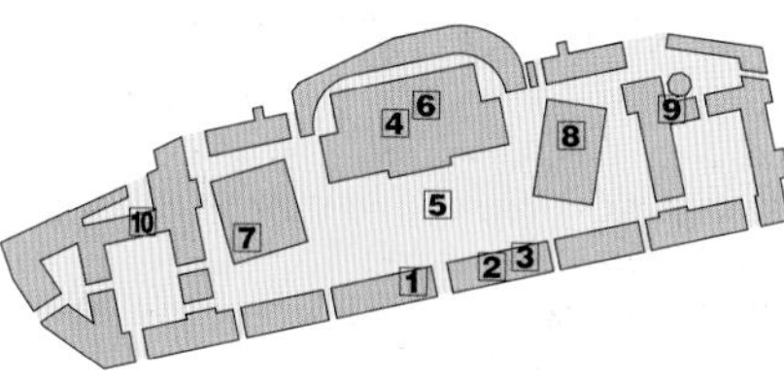

5 Courtyards

The area has six courtyards, but the large main square *(above)* is the most impressive, tiled with white stones.

Plan of the Museumsquartier

9 Architectural Centre Vienna

Hosting changing exhibitions, lectures and symposiums, the Architectural Centre explores building projects in Austria.

10 Zoom Kindermuseum

An exciting place to learn *(above)*, here children are encouraged to explore the world using all their senses through a variety of fun exhibits *(see p67)*.

6 Staircases

Two grand flights of stairs on the left and the right of the Winter Riding Hall lead to the two museums. Further bridges and stairways lead to a viewpoint over the complex.

7 Leopold Museum

The elegant white limestone cube hosts a magnificent collection of Austrian art *(right)*, from Gustav Klimt to Oskar Kokoschka. More than 5,000 artworks were collected by Rudolf Leopold and sold to the Republic of Austria in 1994.

8 Museum of Modern Art

A remarkable collection of contemporary art is housed within this striking building constructed of grey basalt lava.

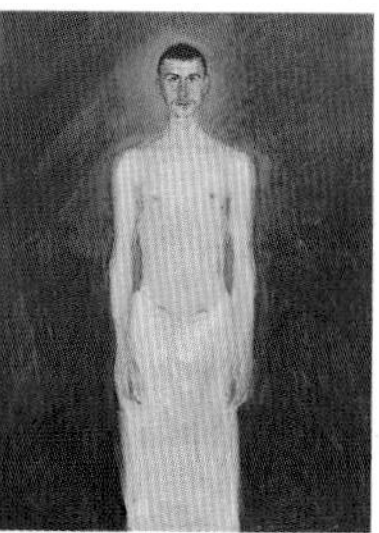

Museumsquartier Guide

The Museumsquartier has 12 entrance gates from all directions, but head for the large main courtyard and pick up a map in the visitor centre. Standing in the main courtyard, the Baroque Winter Riding Hall is just ahead of you, flanked by the white Leopold Museum on the left and the anthracite-coloured MUMOK on the right. The various exhibition spaces and cultural centres are spread around the six courtyards of the complex.

Top 10 Staatsoper

As the first of the grand buildings on the Ringstrasse, construction of the Neo-Renaissance State Opera House began in 1861 under the architects Eduard van der Nüll and August von Siccardsburg, and opened in May 1869 with Mozart's Don Giovanni. *However, the new opera house did not appeal to Emperor Franz Joseph, who referred to it as a "railway station", leading van der Nüll to commit suicide. In 1945 the Staatsoper was hit by World War II bombs and almost entirely destroyed. Fitted with new technology, it reopened in 1955 – a sign that Austria had regained sovereignty from the departing occupying forces.*

Staatsoper exterior

If you don't want to join a guided tour, there is always the possibility of attending a performance in the opera house. Ticket prices range from €3.50 to €178. Standing-room-only tickets can be bought on the day.

- *Opernring 2*
- *Map M5*
- *01 514 44 2250 (tours); 01 513 15 13 (tickets)*
- *www.wiener-staatsoper.at*
- *Open for guided tours several times daily; call for times or check the website for the latest information*
- *Dis. access*
- *Adm €5 (for guided tours) or €6.50, including the State Opera Museum.*
- *State Opera Museum: Hanuschgasse 3/ Goethegasse 1; Open 10am–6pm Tue–Sun*

Top 10 Features

1. Exterior
2. Bronze Statues
3. Fountains
4. Grand Staircase
5. Reliefs of Opera and Ballet
6. Schwind Foyer
7. Gustav Mahler Bust
8. Tea Salon
9. Auditorium
10. Tapestries

1 Exterior

Seen from the Ringstrasse, the majestic stone building is dominated by the original loggia, which survived World War II.

2 Bronze Statues

The bronze statues, placed in the five arches of the loggia, are a creation of Ernst Julius Hähnel (1876) and are allegories of heroism, drama, fantasy, comedy and love, as seen from left to right.

3 Fountains

The two fountains on each side of the opera house were created by Josef Gasser (1817–68). They represent two worlds: music, dance and joy on the left, and the siren Lorelei *(right)* supported by sorrow, love and vengeance on the right.

4 Grand Staircase

The magnificent marble staircase *(above)*, decorated with frescoes, mirrors and chandeliers, leads to the auditorium. Placed in the arches are more statues by Josef Gasser, illustrating the seven liberal arts: architecture, sculpture, poetry, dance, art, music and drama.

For more music venues in Vienna **See pp60–61**

5 Reliefs of Opera and Ballet

Created by Johann Preleuthner, two reliefs show the two genres performed in the house: opera and ballet *(above)*.

Gustav Mahler Bust 7

The bronze bust of the composer Gustav Mahler *(right)*, who was the director of the Vienna Court Opera for 10 years from 1897 to 1907, was created by French sculptor Auguste Rodin in 1909. Mahler's bust is placed in the Schwind Foyer, along with other busts of "conducting directors" who have all worked at the Vienna State Opera House.

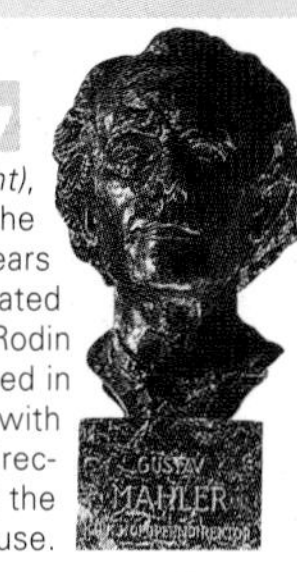

9 Auditorium

The auditorium was rebuilt after World War II, but the basic 1869 design with three box circles and two open circles was maintained.

10 Tapestries

Nine tapestries in the Gustav Mahler Hall, designed by Rudolf Eisenmenger, show scenes from Mozart's opera *The Magic Flute (below)*.

6 Schwind Foyer

In the superb Schwind Foyer *(right)* are 16 oil paintings by Moritz von Schwind representing some famous operas, including Beethoven's *Fidelio* and Rossini's *The Barber of Seville*. A bust of the composers is placed underneath each illustration.

8 Tea Salon

The most splendid room in the house is the Tea Salon. The centrepiece is a fireplace flanked by pillars and mirrors.

Vienna Opera Ball

The highlight of Vienna's social calendar is the Opera Ball, held annually on the last Thursday of the *Fasching* (carnival season). Seats in the auditorium are dismantled to make way for a dance floor where the country's *crème de la crème* waltz the night away. Rooted in a tradition of imperial festivities, the first postwar dance in all its splendour was held in 1956, after the country had started to recover from the years of occupation.

The Vienna State Opera House has seating for 2,880 people; tickets go on sale one week before the performance

TOP 10 Secession Building

The large, white, cubic Secession building was designed by the architect Joseph Maria Olbrich in 1897 as the manifesto of the Secessionist movement (see p25) *and the exhibition hall opened in October 1898. Most of the original interior was looted during World War II and the building was left in a desolate state until the passion for Viennese Art Nouveau was rediscovered in the 1970s and the pavilion rescued from decay. Today it is one of the most treasured examples of a particularly Viennese artistic period.*

Secession building's dome

The café in the building, Café Secession, serves drinks and snacks and has a great terrace outside during the summer months. Alternatively, the Wein & Co Bar just opposite the Secession is a good choice *(see p114).*

- *Friedrichstrasse 12*
- *Map L6*
- *01 587 53 07*
- *www.secession.at*
- *Open 10am–6pm Tue–Sun*
- *Dis. access to main exhibition room and gallery*
- *Adm €9*

Top 10 Features

1. Architecture
2. Façade
3. Dome
4. Motto
5. Ornaments
6. Gorgons' Heads
7. Flower Pots
8. Interior
9. Beethoven Frieze
10. Mark Anthony Statue

1 Architecture

The ground plan of the pavilion reveals simple geometrical forms, taking the square as the basic shape. The framework is softened by curves and ornaments.

2 Façade

The building is quite sober and only uses two colours: white and gold *(right)*. Due to its massive, unbroken walls, the construction has the appearance of being constructed from a series of solid cubes.

3 Dome

The most prominent feature of the otherwise clean design is the dome, made of 3,000 gilt laurel leaves. The laurel symbolizes victory, dignity and purity.

4 Motto

Above the entrance of the pavilion is the motto of the Secessionist movement *"Der Zeit ihre Kunst. Der Kunst ihre Freiheit"* – "To every age its art, to art its freedom" *(below)*.

DER·ZEIT·IHRE·KVNST·
DER·KVNST·IHRE·FREIHEIT·

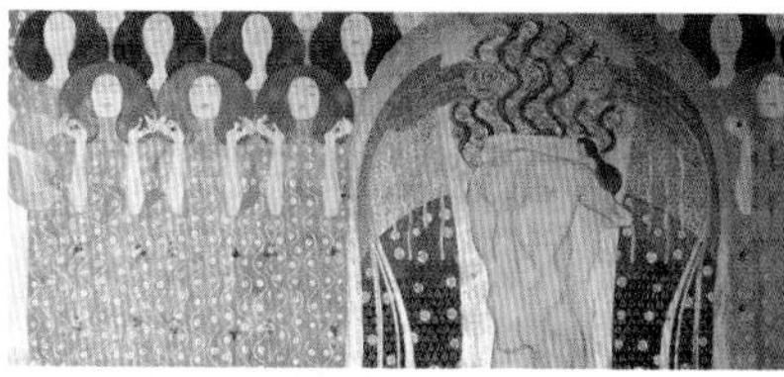

5 Ornaments

The entire building is decorated with gilt laurel garlands, floral patterns and plants along the sides of the walls. But most striking is the tree above the main door which is entirely laid out in gold. These details contrast strikingly with the simplistic façade.

6 Gorgons' Heads

The entrance area is decorated with the heads of the three Gorgons *(below)*, which represent architecture, sculpture and painting. The sides also feature owls, formed by Olbrich himself, and together with the Gorgons they are attributes of Pallas Athena, the Greek goddess of wisdom, victory and the crafts.

7 Flower Pots

The blue mosaic flowerpots on the left and right of the entrance door are carried by four turtles. Small trees add a touch of nature to smooth the building's hard lines.

8 Interior

The exhibition hall, in the shape of a basilica with a lofty nave and two lower aisles, can be easily adapted for each show staged here. It is almost completely covered by a vaulted glass roof that by day bathes the interior in a constant and even light.

9 Beethoven Frieze

Created by Gustav Klimt in 1902 for an exhibition paying homage to Ludwig van Beethoven, the 34-m- (110-ft-) long fresco *(left)* tells a narrative revolving around the composer's Ninth symphony, *Ode to Joy*. Today the frieze is regarded as one of the masterpieces of Viennese Art Nouveau.

10 Mark Anthony Statue

The bronze sculpture of the Roman general Mark Anthony in a chariot drawn by lions *(above)* was created by Arthur Strasser in 1898. It was displayed at the fourth exhibition in the Secession and was then placed outside, to the right of the building.

Unveiling the Secession

The sober functionalism of the Secession building was regarded with horror and widely condemned when it was completed in 1898. Critics claimed it looked like "a greenhouse", "a warehouse" or "a public convenience" and was an assault on good taste. Today, however, it is regarded as one of the key works of the Viennese Art Nouveau style and the Viennese are proud of "their" building, which is affectionately called "the golden cabbage" because of its dome.

TOP 10 Hundertwasserhaus

Opened in March 1986, this fairytale-like house with onion spires, green roof and a multicoloured façade is one of the city's most frequented landmarks. It was designed by the flamboyant Austrian artist Friedensreich Hundertwasser as a playful take on usually dull council (social) housing. In all his work Hundertwasser wanted to show that practical could also be beautiful. Today almost 200 people live in the 50 apartments, each of which has an individual decoration. Shrubs and trees on the balconies and roof gardens bring nature closer to city dwellers.

Hundertwasserhaus façade

Because the apartments are private residences and can't be visited, enjoy the building from one of the several cafés in the complex, and stroll around the shops on the ground floor.

- *Kegelgasse/ Löwengasse*
- *U-Bahn Landstrasse or trams 1 or O to Löwengasse or 4A to Marxergasse*
- *www. hundertwasserhaus.at*
- *Closed to the public*

Top 10 Features

1. Façade
2. Main Entrance
3. Onion Towers
4. Irregular Windows
5. Roof Gardens
6. Ceramic Line
7. Decorations
8. Pillars
9. Glass Front
10. Pavement

1 Façade

The front of the house *(right)* presents itself in bright shades of blue, yellow, red and white and each differently coloured section marks one apartment. What also springs to the visitor's eye are the many trees on the rooftop.

2 Main Entrance

Situated on Löwengasse, the main entrance is an open section leading to the inner courtyard of the building. The apartments above the main entrance are supported by colourful pillars. In front of the entrance is an attractive little fountain *(below)*.

3 Onion Towers

Two golden glistening onion towers top the Hundertwasserhaus and lend the building an Oriental, romantic quality.

4 Irregular Windows

As Hundertwasser believed windows constitute a house's soul, all of them vary in size and shape. Each of them is framed by a complementary colour.

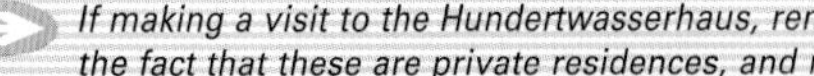

If making a visit to the Hundertwasserhaus, remember to respect the fact that these are private residences, and remain unobtrusive

5 Roof Gardens

Each of the apartments has access to a little piece of nature in the form of roof gardens and balconies that are scattered all over the building. The gardens have some 250 large trees, trimmed shrubs and a grass lawn.

8 Pillars

A prominent feature of the Hundertwasserhaus is the range of brightly coloured, irregularly shaped, shiny pillars *(left)*. Some of these pillars are integrated in the building and function as mere decoration, while others are more practical, supporting the gallery that runs along the first floor of the block.

9 Glass Front

The two towers of the house – those crowned by the onion domes – host the central staircase. Thanks to the glass fronts, by day they are always light and airy.

10 Pavement

The area around Löwengasse *(below)* is pedestrianized with relaxed seating and elegant lampposts.

6 Ceramic Line

The size of every apartment is visible as it is marked by an uneven line of ceramic tiles.

7 Decorations

The Hundertwasserhaus is decorated with various ornaments such as black, white and golden tiles *(left)*. Statues placed on the corners of the balconies, painted animals and plants on the corridor walls, and roof gardens enhance the cheerfulness of the place.

Friedensreich Hundertwasser

When Friedensreich Hundertwasser (1928–2000) left the Vienna Academy of Fine Arts in 1948 after only three months of study, it was hard to imagine that he would become one of Austria's most acclaimed artists and a master of design for everything from buildings to coins, stamps and paintings. Bright colours contrasted by black and gold, and the spiral, symbolizing the beginning and end of life, became his trademarks. His aim was to find harmony between nature and man.

Schloss Schönbrunn

The former summer residence of the Habsburgs, Schloss Schönbrunn (Schönbrunn Palace) was built on land acquired by Maximilian II in 1569. At that time it was a wooded area outside the city. During the Turkish Siege of 1683, however, the woodland was destroyed, leaving the ground free for the construction of this spectacular palace, built between 1695 and 1713 to the designs of the architect Johann Fischer von Erlach. Little of his original plans remain – Empress Maria Theresa ordered most of the interior to be redesigned in Rococo style (see p39)*, and the façade was altered in 1817–19, when it was painted in the characteristic "Schönbrunn yellow".*

Schloss Schönbrunn façade

Of the nine cafés and restaurants on the premises, the café in the Gloriette *(see p38)* offers the best views of the palace and the city.

There are several admission prices and combination passes for the palace and grounds, depending on how many sights you want to visit.

- *Schönbrunner Schloss Strasse 47*
- *U-Bahn Schönbrunn*
- *01 811 13 239*
- *www.schoenbrunn.at*
- *Open Apr–Jun & Sep–Oct: 8:30am–5pm daily, Jul–Aug: 8:30am–6pm daily, Nov–Mar: 8:30am–4:30pm daily*
- *Dis. access*
- *Adm: Imperial Tour €11.50 (22 rooms); Grand Tour €14.50 (40 rooms); Apr–Oct: Classic Pass €18.50, Classic Pass Plus €21.50, Gold Pass €39.90; all year round: Sisi ticket €25.50 (includes Hofburg and Imperial Furniture Museum)*

Top 10 Features

1. Grand Gallery
2. Mirror Room
3. Millions' Room
4. Napoleon's Room
5. Vieux-Laque Room
6. Blue Chinese Salon
7. Empress Elisabeth Salon
8. Porcelain Room
9. Bergl Rooms
10. Chapel

1 Grand Gallery

The 40-m- (130-ft-) long, 10-m- (30-ft-) wide gallery *(right)* has a stunning Rococo design of tall windows, splendid crystal mirrors, chandeliers and white-and-gold stucco. The Grand Gallery is still used for state receptions and banquets.

2 Mirror Room

With its magnificent white-and-gold Rococo decoration and crystal mirrors, this room *(below)* is a fine example of Maria Theresa's style. Mozart once gave a private performance for the empress here.

3 Millions' Room

The name derives from the room's rosewood panelling, which cost a reputed one million Gulden (former Austrian gold coins). In the panels, Indo-Persian miniatures illustrate scenes from the lives of the Mogul rulers of India in the 16th and 17th centuries. Maria Theresa used the room for small audiences.

Plan of Schloss Schönbrunn

4 Napoleon's Room

When Napoleon occupied Vienna in 1805–9 he stayed in this room *(above)*. Eighteenth-century Flemish tapestries adorn the walls.

6 Blue Chinese Salon

Blue wallpaper (made of rice paper), Japanese vases and pieces of lacquer furniture create an Oriental theme here.

8 Porcelain Room

The walls of Maria Theresa's former study are covered with carved wooden frames that are painted blue and white to imitate porcelain.

9 Bergl Rooms

The garden rooms were painted with frescoes by Johann Wenzl Bergl (1768–77) to satisfy Maria Theresa's taste for exotic landscapes. They give an illusion of wild nature. (No longer open to the public.)

10 Chapel

In 1740 Maria Theresa remodelled the chapel. The marble altar *(below)* was designed by Georg Raphael Donner, and Paul Troger painted the ceiling fresco *The Marriage of the Virgin*.

5 Vieux-Laque Room

The interior of this room *(below right)* unites Rococo elements with Chinese art: black lacquer panels from Beijing show landscapes, birds and flowers embellished in gold. After Maria Theresa's husband Franz Stephan died in 1765, she hung several portraits of him here as a memorial.

7 Empress Elisabeth Salon

In Elisabeth's Neo-Rococo reception room, there are portraits of Emperor Josef I as a child and his sister Marie Antoinette.

Palace Guide

Enter through the main gate and head towards the left wing, where you can buy tickets for visiting the interior and pick up a map of the palace and grounds. The carriage museum, greenhouse and zoo are located to the right of the palace *(see pp38–9)*. Behind the palace are the strictly symmetrical Baroque flowerbeds.

The Austrian monarchy ended in 1918 when the last emperor, Karl I, renounced his claim to the throne in the Blue Chinese Salon

Left **Schönbrunn Park** Right **Orangery**

Top 10 Features of Schönbrunn's Gardens

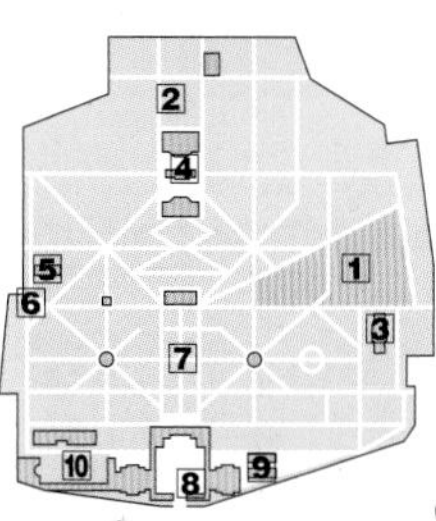

Map of Schönbrunn's Gardens

1 Schönbrunn Zoo

Founded as early as 1752 as a royal menagerie by Emperor Franz I, the Schönbrunn Zoo is the world's oldest zoo and home to some 750 wild and domestic animals.

2 Schönbrunn Park

The formal French Baroque park was laid out as a large pleasure garden by Nicolaus Jadot and Adrian von Steckhoven during the reign of Maria Theresa. It includes various architectural features.

3 Palmenhaus

The impressive steel-and-glass palm house construction was built in 1881–2 by Franz Xavier Segenschmid, using the latest technology of the time to give an appearance that, even today, is light and airy. The central pavilion is 28 m (90 ft) high and has two lateral wings.

Schönbrunn Zoo

4 Gloriette

Situated at the summit of the park's hill, the magnificent Gloriette is its most prominent feature. The arcaded edifice was designed by Ferdinand Hetzendorf von Hohenberg in 1775 in Neo-Classical style and was once used as a dining hall before it became a viewing point, then later a café.

5 Beautiful Fountain

A fresh spring was discovered by Emperor Matthias while hunting in the area in 1619. In 1630, a well, together with a statue of a Roman nymph, was placed here, and eventually gave the palace its name (*Schönbrunn* is German for "beautiful fountain"). The fountain is close to the Roman Ruins.

6 Roman Ruins

Built in 1778, the Roman Ruins were designed to enhance the prestige and image of the Habsburgs by presenting them as the successors to the heroic Roman emperors.

7 Mythological Statues

The large park is dotted with 32 stone statues, created by Christian Beyer between 1753 and 1775. Each one represents a figure in Greek mythology or Roman history.

For more parks and gardens in Vienna **See pp52–3**

8 Schlosstheater
Commissioned by Maria Theresa, the theatre opened in 1747. The empress and her many children performed on the stage as singers.

9 Wagenburg
A highlight of the *Wagenburg* (carriage museum) is the richly decorated imperial coach which was built for the coronation of Josef II in 1764. It was so heavy that eight horses were needed to pull it at walking pace.

A statue in Schönbrunn Park

10 Orangery
The second largest Baroque orangery in the world was once used as winter quarters for orange trees and other potted plants, as well as for various imperial festivities.

Empress Maria Theresa and Schloss Schönbrunn

Most of the palace as it appears today was created during the reign of Empress Maria Theresa. She could only ascend the throne in 1740 after her father Karl VI had declared a change in succession to enable females to take over the rule of Habsburg countries. The early years of her reign were characterized by foreign political failures as parts of Poland and Italy were lost in various wars. But she left an imprint on Austrian domestic politics by introducing compulsory education, establishing a new administrative structure and improving the social situation for farmers. Maria Theresa was impulsive in her younger years, but after the death of her husband Franz Stephan von Lothringen in 1765 she wore only black mourning gowns and lived a sombre existence. She bore 16 children, 10 of whom survived into adulthood.

Top 10 Residents of Schloss Schönbrunn

1. Karl VI (1685–1740)
2. Maria Theresa (1717–80)
3. Franz Stephan von Lothringen (1708–65)
4. Marie Antoinette, wife of Ludwig XVI (1755–93)
5. Napoleon (1769–1821)
6. Marie Louise, wife of Napoleon I (1791–1847)
7. Franz Josef Karl, Duke of Reichstadt (1811–32)
8. Franz Joseph (1830–1916)
9. Elisabeth, wife of Franz Joseph (1837–98)
10. Rudolph (1858–89)

Empress Maria Theresa

Left **October Revolution, 1848** Right **Hitler comes to Vienna to announce the Anschluss**

TOP 10 Moments in History

1 Early Vienna

Early settlements date back to the late Stone Age (5000 BC). The Celts established the kingdom of Noricum in 200 BC. This was conquered by the Romans in 15 BC, who later set up a garrison, Vindobona, in AD 100.

Seal of Rudolf I

2 Babenberg Rule

In AD 976 the Babenberg ruler Leopold was appointed Duke of the Eastern March, and in 1030 the name "Vienna" was mentioned for the first time. In 1156 Vienna became the residence of the Babenbergs and developed into a centre of trade.

3 Habsburg Rule

After the death of the last Babenberg and a period of social disorder, the Habsburg Rudolf I was elected king in 1273. Vienna became the centre of the Holy Roman Empire and remained the imperial city of the Habsburgs until 1918.

4 Turkish Siege

After Turkish troops failed to conquer Vienna in 1529, a 200,000-strong army under Kara Mustafa returned in 1683. The city was held under siege for three months, but with the help of Polish troops it was liberated in September 1683. Prince Eugen finally diminished the influence of the Ottoman Empire with his victory in Belgrade in 1717.

5 Vienna Congress

After Napoleon was defeated in Leipzig (1813), the European powers met in Vienna in 1814–15 to make territorial decisions and create a balance of power. The congress was attended by high-ranking delegates and accompanied by glamorous balls.

6 1848 Revolution

A rigid political system under the state chancellor Metternich led to a period of calm and a rich cultural life (1815–48), but social discontent returned and led to the revolution of 1848. Upheavals reached a peak in the October Revolution. Metternich was ousted from power and a conservative monarchy under Franz Joseph I was installed *(see p15)*.

Failed Turkish Siege of Vienna, 1529

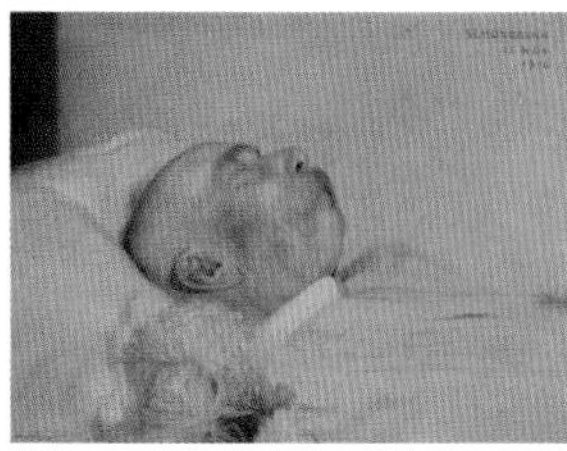
Franz Joseph I on his deathbed

7 End of the Austro-Hungarian Empire

With the death of Franz Joseph I in 1916, the Austro-Hungarian monarchy lost its uniting figure. Karl, his successor, was not able to secure peace. The empire's defeat in World War I resulted in the Habsburgs losing both their lands and their crown.

8 First Republic

When a new European map was drawn in 1918 at the end of World War I, the small Republic of Austria emerged. However, the country was struggling both economically and politically. Social unrest led to a civil war in February 1934, followed by a period of authoritarian rule.

9 Anschluss

In March 1938 Adolf Hitler marched on Vienna and declared Austria part of the Third Reich. Vienna was badly bombed during World War II, with many of its famous landmarks destroyed.

10 Second Republic

In 1945, at the end of World War II, Vienna was divided into four zones occupied by the four Allied powers (Great Britain, France, Russia and the USA). Ten years later the last Allied soldiers left the country, and Austria regained full sovereignty with the signing of the State Treaty in May 1955 *(see p23)*.

Top 10 Emperors and Empresses

1 Rudolf I

Rudolf (1273–91) began the Habsburg rule in Austria.

2 Friedrich III

The motto of Friedrich III (1440–93) was AEIOU – *"Alle Erde ist Österreichs Untertan"* (All Earth Is Austria's Subject).

3 Maximilian I

Under this Renaissance ruler (1486–1519), all Habsburg lands were united and the arts and sciences flourished.

4 Karl VI

Karl VI (1711–40) changed the rules of succession, allowing females to ascend to the throne.

5 Maria Theresa

Maria Theresa (1740–80), known for her strong Catholic beliefs, modernized the empire by introducing many reforms.

6 Joseph II

Known as a tolerant ruler, Joseph II (1765–90) carried out further reforms started under his mother Maria Theresa.

7 Franz II

As the last Emperor of the Holy Roman Empire, the Napoleonic Wars and Vienna Congress came under the reign of Franz II (1792–1835).

8 Ferdinand I

As he was epileptic and physically weak, the country was ruled by Ferdinand's advisors (1835–48).

9 Franz Joseph I

He came to power aged 18 and epitomized the monarchy as no other emperor before him (1848–1916).

10 Karl I

As the last Habsburg monarch (1916–18), Karl I was forced to leave the country in exile in 1918.

Left **Technisches Museum Wien** Right **Haus der Musik**

TOP 10 Museums

1 Kunsthistorisches Museum and Naturhistorisches Museum

The Museum of Fine Arts *(see pp18–21)* and the Natural History Museum *(see p103)* are the two gems of Vienna's world-class exhibition spaces and shouldn't be missed by any visitor.

2 Mozarthaus Vienna

Mozart occupied a flat on the first floor of the Figarohaus in 1784–7. He is said to have been happiest in this residence, and composed some of his masterworks here – the Haydn quartets, a handful of piano concerti and *The Marriage of Figaro*. Restored for Mozart Year in 2006 (Mozart's 250th birthday), it features exhibitions on two upper floors as well as Mozart's first-floor flat *(see p59)*. *Domgasse 5 • Map N3 • Open 10am–7pm daily • Adm • www.mozarthausvienna.at*

Naturhistorisches Museum façade

3 Museum für Angewandte Kunst (MAK)

Designed by Heinrich Ferstel in the Italian Renaissance style, the Austrian Museum of Applied Arts opened in 1871 and is today among Vienna's most exciting exhibitions. The permanent collection, from the Gothic to the present, includes world-famous works by the Wiener Werkstätte, an arts and crafts studio from 1870 to 1956, as well as glassware and lace works. *Stubenring 5 • Map Q3 • Open 10am–10pm Tue, 10am–6pm Wed–Sun • Dis. access • Adm (free Sat and for under 19s) • www.mak.at*

4 Technisches Museum Wien

Opened in 1918, the Vienna Museum of Technology houses more than 80,000 exhibits from the world of technology, energy and heavy industry. The collections include many rarities by Austrian inventors, among them the world's first turbine by Viktor Kaplan (1919) and the first functioning sewing machine by Josef Madersberger (1814). *Mariahilfer Strasse 212 • U-Bahn Schönbrunn; Tram 52, 58 • Open 9am–6pm Mon–Fri, 10am–6pm Sat, Sun & public holidays • Dis. access • Adm (free for under 19s) • www.technischesmuseum.at*

5 Jüdisches Museum der Stadt Wien

The world's first Jewish museum was founded in Vienna in 1895, but the exhibits were confiscated by the National Socialists in 1938. Today's

There is an excellent café in the Jewish museum, Café Teitelbaum, serving kosher food and wine

museum was established in 1990 and shows unique collections of ritual objects, such as Chanukah lamps and Torah crowns. The museum also hosts temporary exhibitions and has a library and archives. ✆ *Palais Eskeles, Dorotheergasse 11 • Map M4 • Open 10am–6pm Sun–Fri • Dis. access • Adm • www.jmw.at*

Tank, Heeresgeschichtliches Museum

6 Wien Museum Karlsplatz

Although the building's post-war exterior doesn't look very inviting, this museum is well worth a visit. Over three storeys Vienna's history is documented with items spanning 7,000 years. Also presented are the lives of famous Viennese as well as paintings by artists such as Gustav Klimt and Egon Schiele. ✆ *Karlsplatz • Map F5 • Open 10am–6pm Tue–Sun & public holidays • Dis. access • Adm (free for under 19s) • www.wienmuseum.at*

7 Haus der Musik

Situated in the historic palace of Archduke Karl, the House of Music opened in 2000 and offers a journey through the world of music. Visitors are invited to experiment with sounds, to play giant instruments or to "conduct" the Vienna Philharmonic Orchestra. ✆ *Seilerstätte 30 • Map N5 • Open 10am–10pm daily • Dis. access • Adm • www.hdm.at*

8 Heergeschichtliches Museum

The Museum of Military History documents the imperial army from the 16th century to the end of the monarchy in 1918. ✆ *Arsenal, Objekt 18 • Bus 69A, 13A; Tram O, D, 18 • Open 9am–5pm daily • Dis. access • Adm (free for under 19s) • www.hgm.or.at*

9 Camera and Photography Museum Westlicht

Around 800 cameras are on display here, including KGB spy cameras disguised as cigarette packets or evening bags. ✆ *Westbahnstrasse 40 • Map E1 • Tram 5, 49 • Open 2–7pm Tue, Wed, Fri, 2–9pm Thu, 11am–7pm Sat & Sun • Dis. access • Adm • www.westlicht.com*

10 Erzbischöfliches Dom- und Diözesanmuseum

This museum is located in the Archbishop's Palace and displays a selection of precious religious art, including liturgical objects. ✆ *Stephansplatz 6 • Map N3 • Open 10am–8pm Tue, 10am–6pm Wed–Sat • Dis. access • Adm*

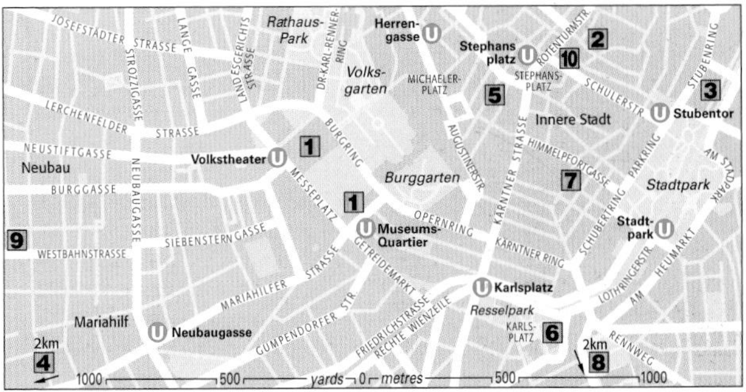

Left **The Belvedere** Right **Albertina façade**

Top 10 Art Galleries

1 Kunsthistorisches Museum

The imperial art collection is housed in the Museum of Fine Arts and includes one of the world's finest gatherings of works by the Old Masters *(see pp18–21)*.

2 The Belvedere

This Baroque palace is home to a wonderful collection of Austrian artworks, including paintings by Klimt and Schiele *(see pp22–5)*.

3 Museumsquartier

Opened in 2001, this complex is home to various museums and galleries, including the Leopold Museum, featuring Austrian art, and the Museum of Modern Art, whose basalt lava building is as impressive as its collections *(see pp28–9)*.

4 Akademie der bildenden Künste

The Academy of Fine Arts has a remarkable collection of 300 masterpieces from the 14th to the 19th centuries. Among them are works by Titian, Van Dyck and Rembrandt, and Hieronymus Bosch's famous Last Judgment triptych (c.1500). There is also a copper etching collection of more than 60,000 works *(see p109)*.

5 Albertina

The Albertina palace is home to a collection of graphic art, architectural drawings and photographs from all periods. The 65,000 drawings and almost one million prints include works by Albrecht Dürer and Gustav Klimt *(see p86)*.

Avenue in the park of Kammer mansion, Gustav Klimt (1912), The Belvedere

6 KunstHaus Wien

Not only is this gallery home to paintings and architectural models by the Austrian artist Friedensreich Hundertwasser, but the colourful building is a work of art in itself. Near the famous Hundertwasserhaus *(see pp34–5)*, the museum's black-and-white façade, uneven floors and roof gardens were designed by the artist in 1989.

Untere Weissgerberstrasse 13 • U-Bahn Landstrasse; Tram O, 1 • Open 10am–7pm daily • www.kunsthauswien.com • Dis. access • Adm

7 Kunsthalle

The Kunsthalle has two venues – one within the Museumsquartier and one at Karlsplatz – thereby offering a large amount of space for changing exhibitions. It specializes in contemporary art, particularly object art. At the Karlsplatz site the exhibits can be seen from the outside, as the building is an airy glass cube.
Ⓢ Museumsplatz 1: Map J5; Open 10am–7pm Fri–Wed, 10am–9pm Thu; Adm • Treitlstrasse 2: Map F4; Open 10am–7pm Fri–Wed, 10am–9pm Thu; Dis. access; Adm • www.kunsthallewien.at

Self-Portrait, Francesco Mazzola (1523–4), Kunsthistorisches Museum

8 Kunstforum Bank Austria

Dedicated to the modern classics and their forerunners, the Kunstforum organizes several major exhibitions a year. By presenting shows of world-famous artists such as Egon Schiele, Oskar Kokoschka, Paul Cézanne, Pablo Picasso and Vincent van Gogh, the gallery is a visitors' magnet and has always attracted large crowds of art lovers.
Ⓢ Freyung 8 • Map L2 • Open 10am–7pm daily (to 9pm Fri) • Dis. access • Adm • www.kunstforumwien.at

9 Künstlerhaus

This edifice was commissioned by the Society of Graphic Artists and built between 1865 and 1868 in the style of the Italian Renaissance. It has changing exhibitions, but there is also the House Gallery, which is mainly used by the society's members to present their works in solo shows. Outside the Künstlerhaus is the Passage Gallery, which offers up-and-coming artists a place to experiment with media and projection art.
Ⓢ Karlsplatz 5 • Map N6 • Open 10am–6pm Fri–Wed (to 9pm Thu) • Dis. access • Adm • www.k-haus.at

10 Museum im Schottenstift

The Scots' Abbey, founded in 1155 by Scottish and Irish Benedictine monks, is a massive complex, with a church, a school and a monastery. The abbey's treasures include tapestries, furniture and liturgical objects, but most important is its religious landscape and portrait paintings from all periods.
Ⓢ Freyung 6 • Map L2 • Open 11am–5pm Thu–Sat (closed public holidays) • Adm

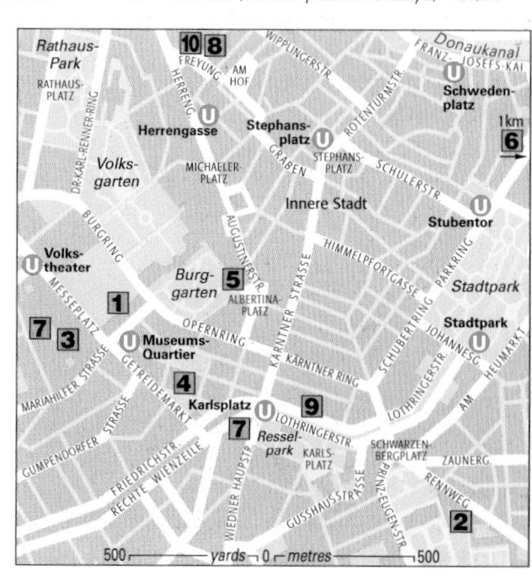

Left **Cemetery grille, Bestattungsmuseum** Right **Coffeepots, Kaffeemuseum**

TOP 10 Unusual Museums

1 Bestattungsmuseum

For the Viennese, death seems to be an extension of life, and funerals are done in style. In the small Undertakers' Museum in Vienna's Zentralfriedhof (Central Cemetery), all kinds of funereal objects are on view. One of the less respectful items is the 18th-century "reusable coffin" – its hinged bottom meant that the corpse could be dropped into the grave, leaving the coffin ready for the next customer. *Zentralfriedhof, Simmeringer Hauptstrasse 234 • Tram 71 • Check website for opening times • Adm • www.bestattungsmuseum.at*

2 Fiaker Museum

The horse-drawn carriages known as *Fiaker* are now largely used by tourists, but they were once the taxis of the city. Photos and models document the history of this Viennese institution. *Veronikagasse 12 • U-Bahn U6 • Open 10am–noon 1st Wed of month • Free*

3 Kriminalmuseum

This museum seeks to shed light on Vienna's darker side and presents the city's most sensational crimes from the Middle Ages to the present. You will find gruesome exhibits here, such as the mummified heads of executed criminals and grisly murder weapons. *Grosse Sperlgasse 24 • Map B5 • U-Bahn U2; Tram 2 • Open 10am–5pm Thu–Sun • Adm • www.kriminalmuseum.at*

4 Schnapsmuseum

A museum devoted to the distilled Austrian drink, Schnapps. The distillery dates to the 1870s but is still used today to produce drinks such as the "Schönbrunn Gold" liquor, made of herb and orange distillates. You can look around the old cauldrons and the office with original furniture – but don't miss the post-tour tasting. *Wilhelmstrasse 19–21 • U-Bahn U6 • Open to groups by appt 9:30am–5:30pm daily (tel. 01 815 73 00) • Dis. access • Adm • www.schnapsmuseum.com*

5 Uhrenmuseum

Located in one of Vienna's oldest houses, this museum has timepieces of all ages and shapes. Items include an astronomical clock from 1769 whose hands take 20,904 years to do a full turn. *Schulhof 2 • Map M2 • Open 10am–6pm Tue–Sun & hols • Adm • www.wienmuseum.at*

Murder scene, Kriminalmuseum

6 Josephinum

The Josephinum houses a unique collection of anatomical wax models that were commissioned by Emperor Joseph II for the training of apprentice surgeons. The medical models were manufactured by Felice Fontana in Florence between 1784 and 1788 and transported on donkeys over mountain passes to Austria. Many medical themes are covered here, but the wax models are the largest collection of its kind in the world *(see p98)*.

7 Pathologisch-Anatomisches Museum

The round "Narrenturm" building, the 18th-century psychiatric ward of the former General Hospital, houses a morbid collection of medical horrors. Begun in 1796 to document pathological changes and malformations of humans, the exhibits include human and animal bones as well as body parts preserved in formaldehyde. ✆ *Vienna University Campus, Spitalgasse 2 • Map B2 • Open 10am–6pm Wed, 10am–1pm Sat • Adm • www.narrenturm.at*

8 Third Man Museum

This museum is privately run and is dedicated to the classic movie *The Third Man*, filmed in Vienna in 1948 during the occupation by the Allied armies. Ten rooms of the museum illustrate the movie's international success and the daily life in postwar Vienna. ✆ *Pressgasse 25 • Map F3 • Open 2–6pm Sat; groups by appointment • Adm • www.3mpc.net*

Original zither used to compose the film's music at the Third Man Museum

9 Circus- und Clownmuseum

Lovers of the Big Top will find plenty to smile about here. The small collection is not only devoted to circus life but also to the art of entertainment, and has props, fancy costumes, historic programmes and colourful circus posters on display. Exhibits also tell the history of famous clowns. ✆ *Ilgplatz 7 • U-Bahn Messe Prater • Open 10am–1pm Sun, 7–9pm 1st & 3rd Thu of each month • Free • www.circus-clownmuseum.at*

10 Kaffeemuseum

This private collection celebrates coffee, the favourite drink of the Viennese. In the little showroom coffee machines from the past 200 years are on display, together with grinders, samovars and coffeepots. There is also the chance to learn about roasting beans. ✆ *Café Benno, Alser Strasse 67 • Map C1 • Open 9am–6pm Mon–Thu, 9am–2pm Fri • Closed Jul–Aug • Dis. access • Free • www.kaffeemuseum.at*

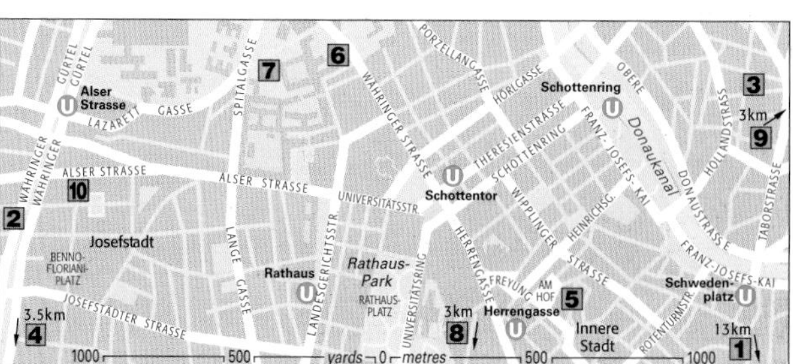

Note: *Children under the age of 14 are not allowed inside the Pathologisch-Anatomisches Museum*

Left **Baroque altar, Michaelerkirche** Right **Painted ceiling, Jesuitenkirche**

Top 10 Places of Worship

1 Stephansdom

Vienna's spectacular Gothic cathedral sits at the heart of the city and dominates the skyline *(see pp8–11).*

2 Karlskirche

This stunning church combines Oriental and Baroque flourishes *(see pp26–7).*

3 Votivkirche

The impressive sandstone church in Neo-Gothic style was built between 1855 and 1879 to express gratitude that Franz Joseph survived an assassination attempt in 1853 *(see p97).*

4 Franziskanerkirche

Located on the charming Franziskanerplatz *(see p90)*, the church and the adjacent monastery of the Franciscan Order were constructed between 1603 and 1611 on the site of an older church. Dedicated to St Hieronymus, it is Vienna's only religious building with a Renaissance façade, but it also bears numerous Gothic as well as Baroque features. These include six side-altars in ornate recesses and a fine Baroque High Altar of 1707 by Andrea Pozzo. *Franziskanerplatz • Map N4*

High Altar statue, Franziskanerkirche

5 Griechisch-Orthodoxe Kirche

In the early 18th century a Greek Orthodox community was founded in Vienna. After a tolerance decree was issued by Emperor Josef II in 1787, the church on Fleischmarkt was built by the Danish architect Theophil von Hansen. The pretty gold-and-red-striped building with arched windows was altered in Byzantine style in the mid-1900s. *Fleischmarkt 13 • Map N2*

6 Michaelerkirche

The imperial court attended masses in this church opposite the Hofburg Palace. Originally Romanesque in style, due to damage by several fires it was changed over the centuries. The original stone helmet of the tower, damaged after an earthquake, was replaced by a pointed roof in 1590. The portal is Baroque (1724–5) and the interior is dominated by Romanesque arcades as well as a Baroque High Altar. *Michaelerplatz • Map M3*

Gothic panel, Maria am Gestade

7 Maria am Gestade

The Gothic church, constructed on the site of a former wooden chapel, has an impressively slim west front, 33 m (108 ft) high and only 10 m (30 ft) wide. The tower is crowned by a white, open stone helmet (1394–1414) that once served as a landmark for Danube mariners. In a state of decay in the late 18th century, it served as horse stables during the Napoleonic wars but was eventually restored in 1812. ⓝ *Passauer Platz • Map M2*

8 Jesuitenkirche

Constructed at the beginning of the 17th century, the solemn façade of the church contrasts with its rich Baroque interior. Emperor Leopold I commissioned the Italian architect Andrea Pozzo to design the magnificent frescoes and paintings. Pozzo also painted the barrel-vaulted ceiling in such a way that the illusion of a dome was created. ⓝ *Dr.-Ignaz-Seipel-Platz • Map P3*

9 Kirche am Steinhof

This fine Art Nouveau church was designed by Otto Wagner and built in 1905–7 on the grounds of a psychiatric hospital. The square-shaped church with two bell towers is overlooked by a golden dome that was converted to copper in the 1930s but more recently restored to its traditional hues. The colourful window mosaics, designed by Kolo Moser, and a gilt altar canopy with angels dominate the interior. ⓝ *Baumgartner Höhe 1 • Bus 47A, 48A • Guided tour 3pm Sat, 4pm Sun • Adm*

10 Wotruba-Kirche

The unconventional church was constructed between 1974 and 1976 following designs by the Austrian sculptor Fritz Wotruba, who died shortly before the work was finished. Situated atop a hill at the edge of the city, it consists of 157 concrete cubes in various sizes that form a harmonious whole. In the spaces between the cubes, glass panes flood the interior with daylight. ⓝ *Georgsgasse, corner of Rysergasse • Bus 60A*

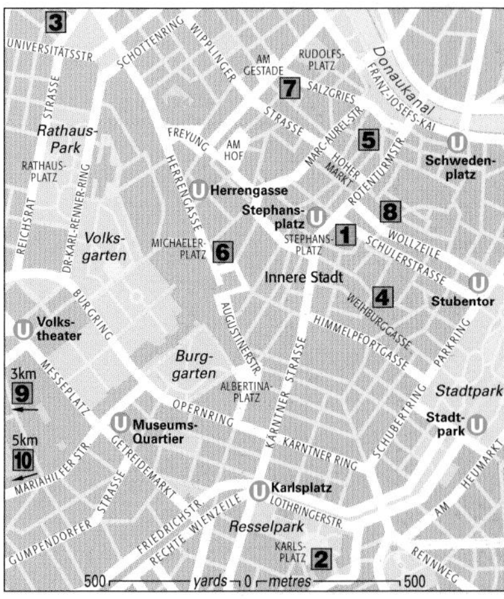

Left **Palais Pallavicini** Right **Augartenpalais**

Palaces and Historic Buildings

1 Palais Liechtenstein

At the end of the 17th century the Liechtenstein family commissioned various architects to build them an impressive Baroque summer residence. It has been renovated and houses the private collection of the Liechtenstein family (mainly 17th-century art) *(see p98)*.

2 Palais Lobkowitz

This large Baroque palace was designed by Giovanni Pietro Tencalla in 1685 as a stately city mansion for Count Dietrichstein. The Lobkowitz family acquired the palace in 1753 and it became known as a music venue where the family's friend Ludwig van Beethoven performed. Today the palace hosts the Austrian Theatre Museum. *Lobkowitzplatz 2 • Map M4 • Open 10am–6pm Tue–Sun • Dis. access • Adm*

3 Palais Pallavicini

Built between 1782 and 1784, the palace was Vienna's first Neo-Classical building, imitating ancient Greek and Roman architecture. The formal façade is enlivened by the impressive portal with caryatids by Franz Anton von Zauner. The owners, the Pallavicini family, still reside here today, and parts of the palace host a congress centre as well as a museum dedicated to the artist Salvador Dalí. *Josefsplatz 5 • Map M4 • Dalí Museum: Open 10am–6pm daily; Dis. access; Adm*

Palais Schönborn-Batthyány

4 Palais Schönborn-Batthyány

The palace, designed by Fischer von Erlach between 1699 and 1706, was the residence of the Hungarian Batthyány family, who fought in Prince Eugen's army *(see p40)*. The Schönborn family acquired it in 1740; today it houses offices. *Renngasse 4 • Map L2 • Closed to the public*

5 Palais Ferstel

This grand building in Historicist style was constructed between 1856 and 1860 by Heinrich Ferstel as a stock exchange for the National Bank. Now part of the palace is the Café Central *(see p94)*, while the courtyard is used as a shopping arcade. *Freyung 2 • Map L2 • Free*

6 Dorotheum

The grand palace in Neo-Baroque style, built between 1898 and 1901 by Emil Ritter von Förster, is home to one of Europe's largest auction houses and pawnshops. Four major auctions are held annually in the numerous showrooms and salons *(see p93)*.

7 Palais Trautson

Count Trautson had this palace built in 1710–17 in French style; Maria Theresa converted it into guards' headquarters in 1760. Today it hosts the Austrian Justice Ministry. *Museumstrasse 7 • Map J4 • Closed to the public*

8 Zeughaus

The 16th-century headquarters of the Vienna fire brigade were remodelled in Baroque style in 1731. The plain façade is contrasted by the pediment with elaborate sculptures. *Am Hof 7 • Map M2 • Open 9am–noon Sun • Free*

9 Augartenpalais

The Baroque palace in Augarten park is now the Vienna Boys' Choir school. *Obere Augartenstrasse 1–3 • Map B5 • Closed to the public*

10 Palais Daun-Kinsky

This is Baroque architect Johann Lukas von Hildebrandt's most splendid palace (1713–16). The Kinsky family purchased it in 1784 and today it hosts various businesses, shops and a restaurant. *Freyung 4 • Map L2*

Palais Daun-Kinsky

Top 10 Architectural Styles

1 Roman Houses

Early houses were built by the Roman garrisons. *Michaelerplatz • Map L3*

2 Medieval House

The Basiliskenhaus is a fine example of a 13th-century home. *Schönlaterngasse 7 • Map P3*

3 Renaissance

The portal of the Salvatorkapelle dates back to 1530. *Salvatorgasse 5 • Map N2*

4 Baroque Palaces

Palaces built in richly decorated Baroque style can be found throughout Vienna.

5 Biedermeier House

Decorated with arabesques and frescoes, this house was built in the 19th century during the Biedermeier age. *Annagasse 11 • Map N5*

6 Art Nouveau Buildings

The stations of the former city railway were constructed by Otto Wagner in the 1890s *(see p117)*.

7 Purist Villa

The symmetrical Villa Moller by Adolf Loos (1917) reflects his principles of the use of space. *Starkfriedgasse 19 • Bus 41A*

8 Council Housing

The massive Karl-Marx-Hof building was constructed in 1930. *Heiligenstädter Strasse 82–92 • U-Bahn U4, U6*

9 Haas-Haus

Built by Hans Hollein in 1990 with a mirrored front *(see p94)*.

10 Gasometer

These 1899 gas storage towers were turned into apartments in 2001. *Guglgasse 8 • U-Bahn U3*

Left **Burggarten** Right **Volksgarten**

TOP 10 Parks and Gardens

1 Schönbrunn Park
The beautiful grounds of the Schloss Schönbrunn include ponds, fountains and a maze *(see pp36–9)*.

2 Stadtpark
The park on the left bank of the River Wien was designed as an artificial landscape within the city in 1862, with paths winding through grassy areas, past ponds and beautiful plantings of shrubs and flowers. But Stadtpark is most famous for the monument of the "King of Waltz", Johann Strauss. ✆ *Parkring • Map P5*

Johann Strauss statue, Stadtpark

3 Augarten
Vienna's oldest park has been open to the public since 1775. Sadly it is now overlooked by the massive anti-aircraft tower built by Hitler's army. However, the formal garden hosts various cultural events during the summer months. ✆ *Obere Augartenstrasse 1 • Map A5*

4 Burggarten
Just behind the National Library is the pretty Burggarten, landscaped in the formal English style and usually inhabited by sun-worshippers on summer days. Located in the large Art Nouveau greenhouse, built in 1901, is a stylish café and restaurant. ✆ *Josefsplatz 1 • Map L5*

5 Volksgarten
This garden, which stretches between the Burgtheater and Heldenplatz, is popular with both students from the nearby university and businessmen on their lunch breaks. It has some beautiful rosebeds that bloom spectacularly in spring. The replica of the Temple of Theseus in Athens is used for a range of changing exhibitions. ✆ *Map K3*

6 Rathauspark
The park in front of the town hall is busy all year round with various festivals, ranging from a Christmas market and an

Rathauspark

ice rink in winter to a summer film and music festival. Many monuments and fountains complement the layout of the park. Another attraction is the large number of centuries-old trees. ⓢ *Map K2*

7 Prater

This large green area just outside the city centre was used as royal hunting grounds until 1766. It is dotted with chestnut trees and is certainly the most popular city park among the Viennese. The lawns and the long avenue are frequented by sunbathers and sports enthusiasts alike. ⓢ *U-Bahn U1 Praterstern*

8 Alpengarten im Belvedere

Established in 1803 by the Habsburg Archduke Johann, this is Europe's oldest alpine garden and is part of the Belvedere park. The beautifully laid-out garden is home to more than 4,000 plants, among them an Oriental bonsai collection *(see pp22–4)*.

9 Tiroler Garten

Archduke Johann so admired the Tyrolean landscape and its alpine architecture that he ordered that an area within Schönbrunn Park be kept as a natural alpine landscape in the 19th century. Today it still boasts an alpine-style house with a small farm and an orchard. ⓢ *Schloss Schönbrunn • U-Bahn U4*

10 Sigmund Freud Park

The green area stretching from Vienna University to the Votivkirche is usually packed with students and picnickers on warm summer days. A ring of different trees surrounding a granite table and chairs represent the member states of the European Union. ⓢ *Universitätsstrasse • Map K1*

Top 10 Fountains

1 Donnerbrunnen

The fountain, created by Georg Raphael Donner in 1737–9, features allegories of Austrian rivers *(see p87)*.

2 Neptunbrunnen

Neptune with his trident overlooks cascades flowing into a large pool. ⓢ *Schloss Schönbrunn • U-Bahn U4*

3 Hochstrahlbrunnen

The enormous fountain, floodlit on summer nights, was built in 1873. ⓢ *Schwarzenbergplatz • Map F5*

4 Vermählungsbrunnen

On the site of the former city gallows, Josef Emanuel von Erlach built a fountain of marble and bronze in 1732. ⓢ *Hoher Markt • Map N2*

5 Andromedabrunnen

The fountain shows the princess Andromeda in the fangs of a sea monster, sculpted by Georg Raphael Donner in 1741. ⓢ *Old Town Hall, Wipplingerstrasse 8 • Map M2*

6 Pallas Athene Brunnen

A statue of the Greek goddess of wisdom towers over the fountain. ⓢ *Dr-Karl-Renner-Ring 3 • Map K3*

7 Danubius Brunnen

Part of the Albertina building, the fountain features allegories of the Danube. ⓢ *Albertinaplatz • Map M5*

8 Michaelerplatz

The monumental fountains of the Hofburg. ⓢ *Map L3*

9 Schutzengelbrunnen

Little dragons spout water beneath the protecting angel who gives the fountain its name. ⓢ *Rilkeplatz • Map F4*

10 Turkish Fountain

The Arabic-style fountain is beautifully tiled. ⓢ *Türkenschanzpark • Tram 41*

Left **Goethe monument** Right **Mahler's grave**

Top 10 Monuments and Memorials

1 Memorial against War and Fascism

The Austrian sculptor Alfred Hrdlicka created a monument in 1988–91 to commemorate all those killed during the National Socialist regime and World War II. Separate elements, made of granite from the area of the Mauthausen concentration camp, are arranged on the square where the Philipphof house was situated. The house was destroyed during an air raid on 12 March 1945 and more than 300 people were buried alive in the debris. The monument includes the Austrian Declaration of Independence on the "Stone of the Republic". *Albertinaplatz • Map M5*

Maria Theresa Monument

2 Maria Theresa Monument

Between the Kunsthistorisches and Naturhistorisches Museums is a statue of Empress Maria Theresa (1717–80). The German sculptor Kaspar von Zumbusch created the monument in 1888, presenting the empress on the throne surrounded by ministers and advisors, as well as composers such as Mozart. *Maria-Theresien-Platz • Map K5*

3 Johann Strauss Monument

Stadtpark is dotted with monuments of Austrian artists and composers, but the gilded statue of Johann Strauss *(see p52)* is allegedly the city's most photographed. The Viennese "Waltz King" is portrayed playing the violin amid ecstatic dancers and is framed by a marble arch. The monument was crafted by Edmund Hellmer in 1921 and has been attracting tourists ever since. *Stadtpark, Parkring • Map P5*

4 Franz Schubert Monument

Another great composer commemorated in Stadtpark is Franz Schubert, seated on a marble base. The monument was commissioned by the men's choir Wiener Männergesangsverein, which specialized in Schubert's songs, and was created by Carl Kundmann in 1872. *Stadtpark, Parkring • Map Q4*

5 Goethe Monument

Next to the Burggarten is a monument to one of the greatest writers in the German language, Johann Wolfgang von Goethe. The statue, seated on a massive base and cast in bronze, was created by Edmund Hellmer in 1900. Opposite the monument is a memorial to another distinguished writer of German literature and Goethe's contemporary, Friedrich Schiller *(see p110)*. *Opernring/Goethegasse • Map L5*

Franz Schubert Monument

6 Mariensäule Am Hof

Am Hof is dominated by a monument to the Virgin Mary that was cast in bronze by Balthasar Herold (1664–7). The base shows four angels fighting four animals, which symbolize the four major catastrophes for humankind in the 17th century. The dragon stands for starvation, the lion for war, the fantastical basilisk for the plague, while heresy is symbolized by a snake. *Am Hof • Map M2*

7 Klimt's Grave

The grave of the leading Secessionist painter Gustav Klimt *(see p25)* is in the Hietzinger Cemetery, close to Schloss Schönbrunn. The simple gravestone bears his name in the way he signed his works of art. He died in 1918 following a stroke. *Hietzinger Friedhof, Maxingstrasse 15 • U-Bahn U4*

8 Schubert's Grave

Franz Schubert was buried at the Währinger Friedhof on 21 November 1828, following his early death aged 31. When the cemetery was closed down in 1872, however, his bones were moved to the Central Cemetery. There he was given an honorary grave among many of his composer friends. *Zentralfriedhof, Simmeringer Hauptstrasse 234 • Tram 71*

9 Schönberg's Grave

Composer Arnold Schönberg (1874–1951), the creator of the 12-tone music technique *(see p59)*, has a striking modern cube as his gravestone, designed by the sculptor Fritz Wotruba. *Zentralfriedhof, Simmeringer Hauptstrasse 234 • Tram 71*

10 Mahler's Grave

Gustav Mahler, the director of the Vienna State Opera from 1897 to 1907, was buried at the Grinzinger Friedhof in 1911. The cemetery is in a peaceful location on the outskirts of the city. Mahler's simple white gravestone was designed by his friend, the architect and designer Josef Hoffmann. *Grinzinger Friedhof, An den langen Lüssen 33 • Train Grinzing*

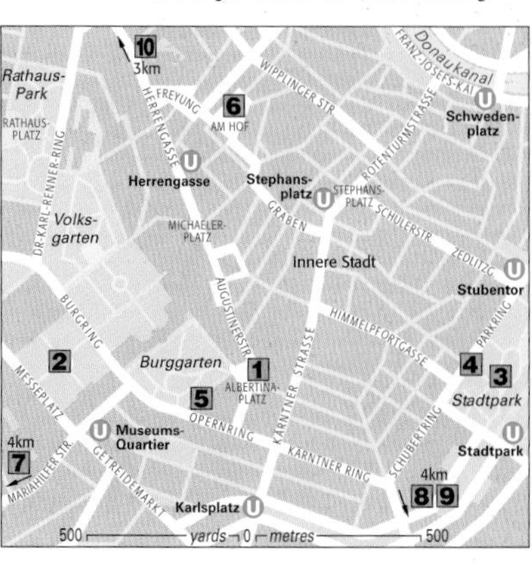

Left **Theater in der Josefstadt** Right **Akademietheater**

Top 10 Theatres

1 Burgtheater

The Burgtheater is one of the most important theatres in the German-speaking world, and the choice of its director at any given period always arouses much political and cultural passion. Premieres of traditional as well as modern plays are closely scrutinized by the public, triggering either enthusiastic or dismissive reactions *(see p85)*.

2 Theater in der Josefstadt

Built in 1788 following the design of Josef Kornhäusel, the theatre was entirely rebuilt in 1822 and reopened with a musical piece by Beethoven, composed for the occasion. It is still very popular today, specializing in classical plays by Austrian writers. *Josefstädter Strasse 26 • Map D2 • Dis. access*

3 Volkstheater

Whereas the Burg, being the Court Theatre, has always been the stage for classical drama, the Volkstheater, or People's Theatre, has aimed at making modern and classic literature accessible to a broader audience since its foundation in 1889. With nearly 1,000 seats, the Volkstheater is among the largest in the German-speaking world *(see p104)*.

4 Akademietheater

The Akademietheater is part of the Konzerthaus building *(see p60)*. Initially it functioned as the training stage for the nearby Academy of Music and Performing Arts, but in 1922 it became the "small" venue for the Burgtheater ensemble. Mainly classic modern plays are staged here. *Lisztstrasse 1 • Map F5 • Dis. access*

Grand staircase, Burgtheater

Note: *All state-funded theatres are closed during the months of July and August*

5 Schauspielhaus

The Schauspielhaus offers a multifaceted programme that includes literary readings and light operas as well as contemporary drama. Since its foundation in 1978, the theatre has seen many Austrian but also world premieres, particularly by the Hungarian-born dramatist George Tabori (1914–2007). It is also one of the many venues for productions by the Wiener Festwochen, Vienna's most important theatre festival *(see p80)*. Being fairly small, the audience has the advantage of being very close to the actors. *Porzellangasse 19 • Map B3 • Dis. access*

6 Raimundtheater

The theatre is named after the Austrian playwright Ferdinand Raimund (1790–1836), as the theatre opened its gates with one of his popular plays in 1893. The Raimundtheater has always specialized in music – after a period of operettas, today it is mainly used as a stage for musicals. *Wallgasse 18–20 • U-Bahn U6 • Dis. access*

7 Vienna's English Theatre

Vienna's English Theatre was founded in 1963 and is the oldest English-language theatre in continental Europe. It was initially intended as a summer venue for tourists but soon extended its programme year-round. The stage has attracted world stars such as Anthony Quinn and Judi Dench to its successful productions. *Josefsgasse 12 • Map D2 • Dis. access*

8 Kammerspiele

This 515-seat theatre was built in 1910 and was first known as the Residenztheater. It is closely connected to the Theater

Schauspielhaus

in der Josefstadt and actors usually perform in different plays in both venues. The Kammerspiele's programme is made up entirely of comedies. *Rotenturmstrasse 20 • Map P2 • Dis. access*

9 Kasino am Schwarzenbergplatz

This is a small and intimate stage, located in a former officers' mess of the imperial army that was adapted as a Burgtheater venue in the 1990s. Its programme includes contemporary plays for a young audience, often followed by debates and talks with the actors. *Schwarzenbergplatz 1 • Map F5 • Dis. access*

10 Rabenhof

The Rabenhof was constructed as council housing for workers in the 1920s, and an assembly hall for the workers' union was built in the basement. This was adapted as a theatre between 1987 and 1992. Today there is a colourful programme of modern plays, comedies and other performances. *Rabengasse 3 • U-Bahn U3 • Dis. access*

Left **Ludwig van Beethoven** Right **Johann Strauss**

Top 10 Composers

1 Wolfgang Amadeus Mozart

Although born in Salzburg, the life of the world-famous composer (1756–91) is inextricably intertwined with Vienna. Mozart moved to the city in 1781 after he had fallen out with his sponsor, the Archbishop of Salzburg. It was here that he wrote his greatest works and celebrated all his triumphs and misfortunes until he died, aged 35.

Wolfgang Amadeus Mozart

2 Ludwig van Beethoven

When Beethoven (1770–1827) gave his first concert in the Vienna Court Theatre in 1795 he already had a reputation as an excellent pianist. Born in Bonn, he moved to Vienna aged 22 to receive tuition from Joseph Haydn and, briefly, Mozart. In 1805 his opera *Fidelio* premiered at the Theater an der Wien *(see p111)*.

3 Joseph Haydn

Along with Mozart and Beethoven, Haydn (1732–1809) is the third important composer of the Vienna Classic period (1770–1830). Haydn moved to Vienna from the countryside, aged eight, to become a choirboy at Stephansdom cathedral. In his house at Haydngasse 19 he wrote his greatest works, such as the oratory *The Creation* (1796–8).

4 Franz Schubert

Schubert (1797–1828) was the twelfth child born in the family home at Nussdorfer Strasse 54. Although he composed many symphonies, it is for his songs that he is best remembered.

5 Johann Strauss

Vienna's "Waltz King" (1825–99) was the most successful of a dynasty of composers and musicians. He wrote more than 500 dance pieces, among them the *Blue Danube Waltz* (1876), which became Austria's unofficial national anthem. He is buried at the Zentralfriedhof *(see p124)*.

6 Johannes Brahms

Brahms (1833–97) was born in Hamburg but became the musical director of the Vienna Singakademie, a choral society, in 1862. For three seasons he directed the Vienna Philharmonic Orchestra, but from 1878 he devoted all of his time to composition. Brahms is also buried at the Zentralfriedhof.

7 **Anton Bruckner**
Born in a small town northwest of Vienna, Bruckner (1824–96) moved to the capital in 1868, when he became a professor at the city's musical academy. Well respected today, his contemporaries were critical about his music and some pieces were never performed during his lifetime.

8 **Arnold Schönberg**
Schönberg (1874–1951) was the founder of the 12-tone serial technique and became one of the most distinguished composers of the 20th century. He left Vienna in 1933 in the wake of National Socialism and died in the US.

9 **Gustav Mahler**
Mahler (1860–1911) composed ten symphonies and song cycles, yet during his lifetime he was better known as a conductor. He was the musical director of the Staatsoper (1897–1907) and led the opera into its golden age.

10 **Alban Berg**
Berg (1885–1935) is known for his operas *Wozzeck* (1925) and the unfinished *Lulu*. During the National Socialist regime, his music was considered indecent and banned from public stages.

Gustav Mahler

Top 10 Mozart's Vienna

1 **Mozarthaus Vienna**
Mozart wrote his opera *The Marriage of Figaro* here. *Domgasse 5 • Map N3 • Open 10am–7pm daily • Adm*

2 **Tiefer Graben**
Mozart stayed at No. 18 on this street during his first concert tour to Vienna in 1762. *Map M2*

3 **Palais Collalto**
The six-year-old Mozart gave his first Vienna concert here in 1762. *Am Hof 13 • Map M2*

4 **Griechenbeisl**
One of the walls in Vienna's oldest inn is adorned with Mozart's signature. *Fleischmarkt 11 • Map P2*

5 **Stephansdom**
Mozart married Constanze Weber on 4 August 1782 in the cathedral *(see pp8–11)*.

6 **Café Frauenhuber**
Mozart gave piano concerts in the music room of the café *(see p94)*.

7 **Mozart's Piano**
Mozart's instrument can be found in the Art History Museum. *Neue Burg • Map L4 • Open 10am–6pm Mon, Wed–Sun • Adm*

8 **Mozart's Grave**
Mozart was buried at the St Marx Cemetery but the site of his grave is unknown. *Leberstrasse • Tram 18*

9 **Mozart Cenotaph**
A cenotaph of Mozart from St Marx Cemetery was relocated to the Zentralfriedhof in 1891. *Simmeringer Hauptstrasse • Tram 71*

10 **Mozartplatz**
Characters from the opera *The Magic Flute* watch over the square. *Map F4*

Left **Staatsoper façade** Right **Theater an der Wien**

Top 10 Music Venues

1 Staatsoper

In a city so intrinsically linked to classical music, no visitor should miss a tour of the spectacular State Opera House *(see pp30–31)*.

2 Musikverein

Public concert life began in Vienna with the foundation of the Society of Friends of Music in 1812; up until then, concerts were restricted to aristocratic homes. This grand concert hall was commissioned by the society in 1869 after previous locations had become too small. The society's aim was, and still is, to promote music in all its facets; until 1909 it also ran a music academy with teachers such as Anton Bruckner and eminent students such as Gustav Mahler *(see p59)*. The school was the predecessor of the present Academy of Music *(see p117)*.

3 Konzerthaus

The Vienna Concert House was opened in 1913 by Emperor Franz Joseph I and the design, by Ferdinand Fellner and Hermann Helmer, is clearly influenced by Art Nouveau style. With four concert halls, over 3,100 seats, and a diverse programme, including contemporary and classical music and jazz, the Konzerthaus attracts music lovers from various camps. *Lothringerstrasse 20 • Map P6 • Dis. access*

4 Volksoper

The "People's Opera" opened in 1898 after a group of industrialists had raised funds to celebrate Franz Joseph's Golden Jubilee, and the façade of the theatre has remained unchanged. Light operas and operettas are performed here, as well as dance productions. *Währinger Strasse 78 • Map A2 • Dis. access*

Volksoper

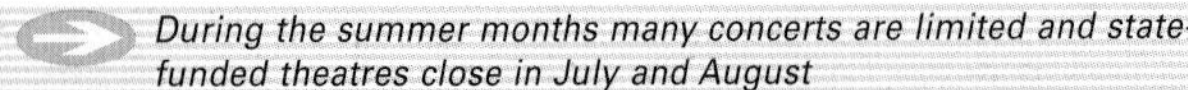

During the summer months many concerts are limited and state-funded theatres close in July and August

5 **Kammeroper**
The Kammeroper, founded in 1954, is dedicated to promoting young singers. The five main productions a year include classic and Baroque operas, as well as some contemporary operas. The Kammeroper is now a subsidiary venue of the Theater an der Wien. *Fleischmarkt 24 • Map P2*

6 **Theater an der Wien**
Having been a musical venue for many years, this historic theatre is once again a working opera house *(see p111)*.

7 **Ronacher**
The original Ronacher, built in 1870, staged tragedies and comedies, but after it burned down in the 1880s architects Ferdinand Fellner and Hermann Helmer replaced it with a variety theatre. Neglected after World War II, the Ronacher reopened in 1988 with the musical *Cats*. *Seilerstätte 9 • Map N4 • Dis. access*

8 **Porgy & Bess**
One of the top jazz clubs in town is mainly dedicated to modern jazz. Alongside star names, many newcomers also get the chance to play. *Riemergasse 11 • Map P4 • Dis. access*

9 **Jazzland**
Another jazz club, this time traditionally orientated. Since its foundation in 1972, international and national artists have been performing in the cellar venue. *Franz-Josefs-Kai 29 • Map P2*

10 **RadioKulturhaus**
The RadioKulturhaus offers a programme of jazz and classical concerts, literary readings and films. Most of the concerts are broadcast on the radio station Ö1. *Argentinierstrasse 30a • Map G5*

Top 10 Nightclubs

1 **U4**
Next to the U4 stop Meidlinger Hauptstrasse, U4 hosts theme nights from boogie to classic rock. *Schönbrunner Strasse 222 • U-Bahn U4*

2 **B72**
This trendy club in the arcades of the U6 metro plays electronic music. *U-Bahnbogen 72–3 • U-Bahn U6*

3 **Volksgarten**
Everything from tango to Havana nights. *Volksgarten park, Dr-Karl-Renner-Ring • Map K4*

4 **Eden Bar**
This tiny cellar bar is a popular meeting point for Vienna's high society. *Liliengasse 2 • Map N4*

5 **Rhiz**
Also in the arcades of the metro, Rhiz has a daily DJ line-up of electronic music. *U-Bahnbögen 37–8 • U-Bahn U6*

6 **Flex**
Underground club with a lively indie scene. *Augartenbrücke • Map B4*

7 **Chelsea**
Live bands and indie music under the U6 metro line. *Lerchenfelder Gürtel, U-Bahnbögen 29–30 • U-Bahn U6*

8 **Escalera**
Classy dance venue, so dress to impress. *Stadtbahnbögen 181-182 • Map A2 • U-Bahn U6*

9 **Arena**
Located in a former slaughterhouse, the music ranges from punk to indie. *Baumgasse 80 • Bus 77A*

10 **Titanic**
Spread over two floors, the music is mainly house, funk and hip-hop. *Theobaldgasse 11 • Map F3 • U-Bahn U3*

Every other day between 2pm and 5pm, theatre tickets are reduced by 50 per cent at the ticket booth next to the Staatsoper

Left **Sewers** Right **Kapuzinergruft**

TOP 10 Underground Vienna

1 Sewers

Vienna's sewers came to fame in the 1949 film classic *The Third Man*, when Harry Lime, played by Orson Welles, was chased through the city's underworld by the police. Filmed in the rubble of postwar Vienna, *The Third Man* is still remembered today, as several tours follow in the footsteps of the characters. *Third Man Walking Tour from Stadtpark U4: 4pm Mon & Fri; Tours of sewers from Esperantopark: May–Oct: 10am–8pm Thu–Sun • www.thirdmantour.at • Adm*

2 Kapuzinergruft

The crypt beneath the Kapuzinerkirche (Capuchin church) was established by Empress Anna in 1618 and served as the Habsburgs' burial place for over 350 years. Among the 146 bodies resting in elaborately decorated sarcophagi or simple coffins are 12 emperors and 19 empresses. However, their hearts were buried separately in silver containers in the crypt of St Augustin's Church *(see entry 8 opposite)* and their intestines in copper urns in the catacombs of the Stephansdom. *Tegetthoffstrasse 2 • Map M4 • Open 10am–6pm daily • Adm*

3 Stephansdom Catacombs

In the 18th century many graveyards were closed down as plague epidemics spread quickly in the densely populated cities. Cemeteries were relocated beneath city churches, and bones were disinterred and reburied in the crypts. The catacombs underneath Stephansdom were constructed after Emperor Karl VI issued a decree to close the cathedral's graveyard in 1732. Today it is hard to imagine that the Stephansplatz was once crammed with gravestones *(see p9)*. *Stephansplatz • Map N3 • Open 10–11:30am & 1–4:30pm Mon–Sat, 1–4:30pm Sun & public holidays • Adm*

Michaelerkirche crypt

4 Michaelerkirche Crypt

This crypt contains well-preserved mummies, some still wearing Baroque frocks and wigs. From 1631 to 1784, some 4,000 bodies were buried here, including nobles who wanted to rest close to the emperor at Hofburg *(see p48)*. *Michaelerplatz • Map M3 • Guided tours 11am & 1pm Mon–Sat (Thu–Sat Nov–Mar), by prior arrangement (tel. 0650 533 80 03) • Adm*

5 Roman Ruins

Remains of the Roman camp Vindobona *(see p40)* can be seen at this underground museum. Excavations show archaeological finds such as pottery and coins. *Hoher Markt 3 • Map N2 • Open 9am–6pm Tue–Sun • Adm*

Roman ruins

6 Vienna Art Cult Centre Schottenstift

The Scots' Abbey on Freyung has widespread vaults that were continually expanded after its foundation in 1155. The storage rooms and wine cellars bear remains from the Romanesque, Baroque and Biedermeier periods. Today the area is used as an exhibition space of the Art Cult Centre *(see p45)*.

7 Virgilkapelle

The large Gothic St Virgil's Chapel was only discovered in the 1970s, when the Vienna metro line U1 was constructed – it had been hidden underground for some 200 years. The foundations of the crypt are visible on the square. Built in 1250, it was originally used for public burials, until a Vienna merchant turned it into his private crypt in the 14th century.

Stephansplatz U-Bahn station • Map N3 • Open 10am–1pm & 2–6pm Tue–Sun & public holidays • Adm

8 Augustinerkirche

St Augustin's Church was built in 1327 in Gothic style. In the course of its history, many imperial weddings took place here, including Marie Louise's marriage to Napoleon in 1810 and Franz Joseph I and Sisi's wedding in 1851. But the church is most famous for its Herzerlgruft (hearts' crypt) containing the hearts of Austria's emperors.

Augustinerstrasse 3 (entrance on Josefsplatz) • Map M4 • Open 8am–6pm daily • Adm

9 Wine Cellars

In the Middle Ages most of Vienna's houses had as many storeys below ground as they had above. The cellars stored vats of wine, vegetables and other goods, and in some cases stables. In times of war the Viennese even lived in these cellars. This extensive underground labyrinth was often connected by tunnels. Many of the cellars were destroyed during the construction of the metro system and numerous underground car parks, but some remain as "*Keller*" (cellar) restaurants, such as Rathauskeller at Wipplingerstrasse 8 and Esterhazykeller at Haarhof 1.

10 Cabaret Fledermaus

A long staircase leads down to the Cabaret Fledermaus, named for the bats *(Fledermäuse)* that would have inhabited Vienna's cellars in the Middle Ages. Today it is frequented by night owls who invade the red velvet interior as one of the major party spots in town. There are events Wednesday to Sunday. *Spiegelgasse 2 • Map M4*

Cabaret Fledermaus sign

Left **Organic products, Freyung** Right **Fresh vegetables, Naschmarkt**

Top 10 Markets and Department Stores

1 Naschmarkt

Unmissable for any visitor interested in busy, colourful markets. Everything from fruit and vegetables to a Saturday flea market *(see p109)*.

Am Hof market

2 Am Hof

The Baroque Am Hof square, with its unique architectural surroundings and cobbled streets, is the perfect setting for an antiques market. Vendors offer all kinds of antique goods on Fridays and Saturdays, but the market is best known for its selection of secondhand books – you might be lucky and find a rare or early edition of your favourite title. *Map M2*

3 Freyung

This city-centre zone has always been an important square for public life. Whereas in medieval times both festivals and executions took place on the Freyung, it is largely markets that are held here today. A little farmers' market selling mainly organic products takes place every two weeks – don't miss out on tasty cheeses, crisp brown bread or smoked ham. But the square really comes to life just before Christmas, when a bustling festive market sells all sorts of handmade art objects and vendors offer alcoholic punch. It also has a picturesque Easter market. A real Viennese experience *(see p80)*. *Map L2*

4 Karmelitermarkt

A daily market takes place on the square encircled by these four streets. It's a colourful, multicultural spot where you can buy vegetables, fruit, groceries and Turkish food, observe traditional Austrian butchers selling fresh poultry, red meat and horse meat, and investigate kosher butchers and grocery shops. However, the market is most interesting at weekends, when farmers and vendors come from outside Vienna to set up their tables and sell their produce. *Im Werd, Krummbaumgasse, Leopoldsgasse & Haidgasse • Map C5*

5 Rochusmarkt

Just outside the Rochusgasse metro station is the small Rochus market. Some 30 permanent stalls offer mainly fruit, vegetables, flowers and fresh meat, but on Saturdays the lively Rochusmarkt increases to almost double the size, when farmers from further afield also come to offer their delectable home-grown crops. *Landstrasser Hauptstrasse • Map R4*

Gasometer

labels, from fashion accessories to home decor and furniture. There is a sushi restaurant and a café on the top floor, both offering an excellent view over the bustling shopping street down below *(see p110)*. ✎ *Mariahilfer Strasse 38–48 • Map F2 • Dis. access*

6 Gasometer

These four round-shaped industrial buildings were constructed in 1899 to store gas. No longer needed for their original purpose, four renowned architects (Coop Himmelblau, Jean Nouvel, Manfred Wehdorn and Wilhelm Holzbauer) converted the massive buildings in 2001 into a shopping centre, an events' hall, 615 apartments and a students' hall of residence. Around 70 shops offer everything from fashion to electronic goods – the separate Gasometer buildings are connected by glazed corridors *(see p51)*. ✎ *Guglgasse 8 • U-Bahn U3 • Dis. access*

7 Wien Mitte The Mall

This spacious, modern shopping mall is located at Wien Mitte station. You'll find every kind of goods here, from fashion clothing labels to shoe shops, electronic items to jewellery, as well as a supermarket which is also open on Sundays. There are cafés and restaurants aplenty at which to rest your feet after a long day's shopping. ✎ *Landstrasser Hauptstrasse 1b • Map R4 • Dis. access*

8 Gerngross

One of Vienna's largest department stores, Gerngross's goods range from designer clothing to middle-of-the-range

9 Steffl

This major department store is located in the heart of the city. You'll find mainly designer names such as Ralph Lauren and Calvin Klein on its five floors, but there are also perfumes, cosmetic products and home decor items on sale. The top floor has great views over the rooftops and the Sky Bar offers excellent cocktails. ✎ *Kärntner Strasse 19 • Map N4 • Dis. access*

10 Ringstrassen Galerien

This elegant shopping centre is Vienna's most expensive retail area, with designer clothes as well as jewellery and gourmet food. The shops are interspersed with cafés and restaurants. ✎ *Kärntner Strasse/Kärntner Ring • Map M6 • Dis. access*

Ringstrassen Galerien

Above **Schloss Schönbrunn**

Top 10 Children's Attractions

1 Schönbrunn Zoo

Considered the oldest zoo in the world, all the usual favourites can be found here, including elephants, reptiles and butterflies. Most are housed in Baroque-style compounds *(see p38)*.

Maze, Schönbrunn Park

2 Schönbrunn Park

Schönbrunn Park is home to two special attractions – the maze and the labyrinth in the palace's gardens. The maze is based on the original 18th-century designs and, once you have made your way through the hedges, there is a viewing platform over the area. The labyrinth is a games area with a giant kaleidoscope, a climbing pole and fun riddles *(see p38)*. *U-Bahn Schönbrunn • Open 9am–5pm daily • Dis. access • Adm*

3 Marionettentheater Schönbrunn

The puppet theatre in the little court theatre at Schönbrunn stages wonderful shows that delight both children and adults. A version of Mozart's *The Magic Flute* is the undisputed highlight of the programme, with a feather-clad Tamino and a spectacularly vicious snake. *Hofratstrakt, Schloss Schönbrunn • U-Bahn Schönbrunn • 01 817 32 474 • Dis. access • Adm • www.marionettentheater.at*

4 Riesenrad

The Vienna Riesenrad, the giant Ferris wheel, is over 100 years old and offers a breathtaking view over Vienna's rooftops. As well as the ride, don't miss the little museum in the entrance area, where the history of both the wheel and the city are displayed in some of the Riesenrad's old red cabins. *Prater 90 • U-Bahn Praterstern • Open Jan, Feb, Nov & Dec: 10am–7:45pm daily; Mar, Apr & Oct: 10am–9:45pm daily; May–Sep: 9am–11:45pm daily • Dis. access • Adm • www.wienerriesenrad.com*

5 Technisches Museum Wien

A special adventure area here, geared towards children aged three to six years old (although older children enjoy it too), allows young visitors to experience the natural sciences with hands-on displays. Children are particularly invited to take part in and carry out various technological experiments. Special workshops in the museum's kindergarten take place between 1pm and 6pm on Tuesdays, Fridays and Saturdays, as well as from 10am to 6pm on Sundays; these are free of charge. This is a great museum for inquisitive little minds *(see p42)*.

The Riesenrad became world-famous when Orson Welles met his opponent in one of its cabins in the film classic The Third Man

Riesenrad

6 Zoom Kindermuseum

This museum is designed exclusively for children and is a place of playful enquiry, learning and discovery. Hands-on exhibitions for toddlers, kitchens for cooking experiments and the chance to "zoom" in on new situations to grasp the world around them are just some of the highlights. Booking ahead recommended. *Museumsplatz 1 • Map K6 • 01 524 79 08 • Dis. access • Free (but fee payable for some activities)*

7 Haus des Meeres

Fish and reptiles from all across the world have found a home in a former anti-aircraft tower in Esterhazypark. You can "journey" from the chilly North Sea to the Australian Great Barrier Reef, taking in the natural landscape en route. Very popular with kids are the sharks' and piranhas' feeding time in the "Amazon pool", and stroking harmless snakes. *Esterhazypark • Map F2 • Open 9am–6pm daily (until 9pm Thu) • Dis. access • Adm*

8 Schloss Schönbrunn

Probably the most exciting guided tours for kids are offered in Schönbrunn Palace. The young visitors are shown the imperial way of life in the palace from a child's perspective and given the chance to learn what a child's life in the imperial family was like. In the Court Bakery they can watch confectioners preparing cakes and pastries – the piping-hot cakes can be sampled fresh from the oven *(see pp36–9)*.

9 Schmetterlinghaus

The large greenhouse in the Burggarten houses more than 150 species of tropical butterflies and moths, living in habitats replicating their natural environment. *Burggarten, Burgring • Map L5 • Open Apr–Oct: 10am–4:45pm Mon–Fri, 10am–6:15pm Sat, Sun & public hols; Nov–Mar: 10am–3:45pm daily • Dis. access • Adm*

10 Adventure Swimming Pool Diana-Tropicana

There are several adventure pools in Vienna, but the Diana-Tropicana is the only one that features dinosaurs and pirate ships. A water slide that also goes upwards is great fun, too. *Lilienbrunngasse 7–9 • Map P1 • Open 10am–10pm Mon–Sat & public holidays, 9am–8pm Sun • Adm*

Zoom Kindermuseum

For family-friendly hotels in Vienna **See p147**

Above **Prater park**

TOP 10 Walks

1 Spittelberg

This picturesque area of cobbled streets makes a lovely stroll year-round, but perhaps the best time is at the run-up to Christmas, when handicrafts and mulled wine are sold at the market *(see p104)*.

2 Alte Donau

The Danube formed an extensive landscape of small islands before it was regulated into a man-made bed in 1870 to prevent flooding. One of the former tributaries, the Alte Donau (Old Danube), now has 11 *Strandbäder* (island beach resorts), including *Gänsehäufel*, the largest outdoor swimming area in Europe. *U-Bahn Alte Donau • www.alte-donau.info*

3 The Danube Canal

The river that runs around the edge of the city centre is not the actual Danube, but one of its many arms, the Danube Canal. Along the promenade, popular with walkers, cyclists and in-line skaters, there is a lively pub and restaurant scene. *U-Bahn Rossauer Lände*

4 Donauinsel

When a large canal, known as the New Danube, was constructed in 1975 to further prevent flooding, the city fathers created a huge recreational island, and in summer the Viennese flock here to make use of cycle paths, and barbecue and swimming areas. The Copa Cagrana, around the U-Bahn stop, offers an abundance of cafés and restaurants. *U-Bahn Donauinsel*

5 Prater

The former imperial hunting grounds are today an expansive park, opened to the public in 1766. Within the park is a pleasure pavilion, two race courses, and the Wurstelprater amusement park with its famous Ferris wheel, the Riesenrad *(see p66)*. *www.prater.vienna.info*

6 Lainzer Tiergarten

This huge area on the western fringe of Vienna contains more than 80 km (50 miles) of walking paths, meadows and playgrounds. The imperial family used the land as hunting grounds from 1557, and the park opened to the public in 1919. Wild boar and deer roam free here. *U-Bahn Hütteldorf • Open mid-Feb–mid-Nov*

Lainzer Tiergarten

No cars are allowed on the Donauinsel, so you will need to take the U-Bahn

Kahlenberg

7 Inner City

The most popular walk in the city centre is the Kärntner Strasse and Graben area, but you'll be surprised to find quiet squares and peaceful courtyards just off the main route.

8 Kahlenberg

Kahlenberg and neighbouring Leopoldsberg, with wonderful views of the city, are popular for Sunday excursions. From Kahlenberg's 425-m (1,395-ft) peak you can even spot the Carpathian Mountains on a clear day *(see p124)*.

9 Wilhelminenberg

Part of the Vienna Woods, Wilhelminenberg is a huge green area with many hiking paths, including one with signs explaining the local flora and fauna. On top of the hill is Schloss Wilhelminenberg, now a hotel. There is also an observatory here. *U-Bahn Ottakring, then Bus B46 or B146*

10 Mariahilfer Strasse

A large section of the city's main shopping street has been pedestrianized, offering lots of space for strolling, and there are many cafés where you can stop to rest your feet *(see p110)*.

Top 10 Outdoor Activities

1 Walking

Besides walking from sight to sight, you can make use of hundreds of hiking paths that weave through the Vienna Woods *(see p124)*.

2 Football

This is the favourite pastime for many Viennese. The Prater and Donaupark are the main venues.

3 In-line Skating

An extremely popular sport, especially at the Prater, where there are hire shops, long flat paths and skating parks.

4 Jogging

It is safe to jog in Vienna, even at night. There are also frequent races for enthusiasts.

5 Cycling

Cycle paths through the city cover more than 800 km (500 miles). The Donauinsel in particular is great for cyclists.

6 Swimming

There are many outdoor as well as indoor pools, and the Danube tributaries are always free to use.

7 Tennis

Former Austrian aces Thomas Muster and Barbara Schett have created plenty of enthusiasm at the city's courts.

8 Golf

If you have a membership card from your home club, you can book a game at one of the three city courses.

9 Mountain Biking

The Kahlenberg and Leopoldsberg hills are ideal for energetic cyclists.

10 Climbing

The anti-aircraft tower in Esterhazypark has a huge climbing wall run by the Austrian Alpine Society.

Left **Frittatensuppe** Right **Gemischter Salat**

10 Viennese Dishes

1 Leberknödelsuppe

Austrians are fond of their soups and a traditional three-course Sunday lunch will often start off with a bowl of clear beef broth. This variety, with little liver dumplings, is undoubtedly the king among Austrian soups.

2 Frittatensuppe

Most soups are made of clear beef stock and are served with a range of garnishes to create some variety. *Frittaten* – pancakes seasoned with a sprinkle of fresh herbs, cut into thin strips and served in bouillon – are a popular option.

3 Tafelspitz

Meat is essential to Viennese cuisine, and beef has played an important role throughout the centuries. The favourite among the many variations is boiled rump, usually served with *Rösti* (fried grated potatoes) and apple and horseradish sauce. Emperor Franz Joseph allegedly ate *Tafelspitz* every day.

4 Wiener Schnitzel

The roots of the *Wiener Schnitzel* lie in ancient Byzantium, where meat was purportedly eaten after being sprinkled with gold. Over the course of time the precious metal was replaced by a coat of golden breadcrumbs. Count Radetzky, who fought several wars for the Austrian Empire in the 19th century, is said to have brought the dish to imperial Vienna from Milan. The outcome is tasty veal or pork covered in breadcrumbs and fried until golden. Potato salad is the classic side dish.

Wiener Schnitzel

5 Gulasch

This dish is the result of a successful symbiosis between Austrian and Hungarian cuisine. The original Hungarian soup-like dish made its way into Viennese kitchens and emerged as *Gulasch* – a spicy beef stew, seasoned with paprika and served with dumplings or bread rolls. There are many variations of the dish, such as *Gulasch* with potatoes or *Gulasch* served with a fried egg and gherkins.

6 Gefüllte Paprika

Stuffed peppers are another remnant of the Austro-Hungarian monarchy, when Vienna was the melting pot of many nationalities and cultures. Originally from the Balkans, the dish quickly became accepted by the Viennese and, just like *Gulasch*, it can now be found in restaurants throughout the city. Green

Gefüllte Paprika

peppers are stuffed with a mixture of minced meat and rice and are usually served with a tomato sauce and potatoes.

7 **Schweinsbraten mit Semmelknödel**
Roast pork is another standard of Viennese cuisine. Seasoning ranges from garlic to fresh herbs and caraway, and the meat is generally served with dumplings, salad and gravy.

8 **Zwiebelrostbraten**
Slices of roast beef are topped with fried onion rings and served with mashed or roasted potatoes. A variation is *Vanille-rostbraten*, in which the meat is seasoned with garlic.

9 **Frankfurters**
The takeaway sausage stall, or *Würstelstand*, is to be found all over Vienna. Slim, pale sausages were introduced to Vienna in 1798 by the butcher Johann Georg Lahner, who named them after the city of Frankfurt from which they came. They are usually served with mustard and a *Semmel* (bread roll).

10 **Gemischter Salat**
Any eatery, be it a little inn or a luxury restaurant, will serve mixed salads to accompany meat dishes. They usually consist of potatoes, lettuce, carrots and tomatoes, arranged side by side.

Top 10 Drinks

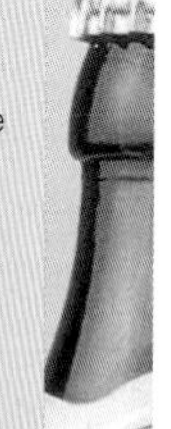

1 **White Wines**
Austria's superb sweet dessert wines are among the world's best. Vienna is the only capital in the world that produces wine. The main varieties are Grüner Veltliner and Weissburgunder.

2 **Red Wines**
Austria's excellent red wines include Zweigelt, Blaufränkisch and Blauer Portugieser.

3 **Gespritzter**
Sparkling water mixed with table wine is an all-time favourite in Austria, particularly in summer.

4 **Sparkling Wines**
The Austrian sparkling wine Sekt is increasingly popular.

5 **Beers**
Several breweries in Vienna produce good, malty beers. Bars and restaurants usually offer a *Seidl* (0.33 litre) or a *Krügel* (0.5 litre).

6 **Soft Drinks**
Apple juice and grape juice mixed *(gespritzt)* with sparkling water is popular, as is *Almdudler*, a herbal lemonade.

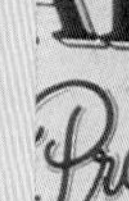

7 **Sturm**
For a few weeks in autumn fermenting grape juice is available. Although it tastes sweet, it is alcoholic and quite powerful.

8 **Schnapps**
A distilled eau de vie made from fruits such as apricots or juniper berries.

9 **Hot Drinks**
Besides coffee *(see p77)*, you will find hot chocolate and tea on offer in cafés.

10 **Mulled Wines**
Around Christmas, hot spicy wine and punch are warming and very popular.

Left **Sachertorte** Right **Dobostorte**

TOP 10 Viennese Cakes

1 Sachertorte

The fact that two famous Vienna confectioners, Sacher and Demel, fought a seven-year legal battle over who had the original recipe for *Sachertorte* shows how seriously the Austrians take their cakes. This rich cake, covered with apricot jam then coated with chocolate, was allegedly invented by Franz Sacher in 1832 and was a taste sensation that conquered the globe. Although every cookbook includes a recipe, the original is top secret.

2 Gugelhupf

With almonds, cocoa or chocolate icing, this cake has numerous variations – its name refers to its characteristic shape, baked in a fluted ring mould. Legend has it that Emperor Franz Joseph had a piece of *Gugelhupf* every time he visited his mistress, the actress Katharina Schratt, for afternoon coffee. The cake is popular for breakfast as well as during the day.

Apfelstrudel

3 Apfelstrudel

Strudel is an essential part of Austrian cuisine. The *Strudel* dough has to be very thin and is then sprinkled with sliced apples, cinnamon, raisins and icing sugar. *Strudel* is served either warm or cold and is eaten both as a dessert and as a main dish in Austrian homes.

4 Dobostorte

Named after its inventor, the Hungarian confectioner Lajos Dobos, this delight requires dedication and experience to prepare. Eight separate layers of light sponge cake are joined together with chocolate cream, while the top layer, glazed with caramel and cut into segments, forms the decoration.

5 Linzertorte

Named after the Austrian city of Linz, this cake has been popular for nearly 300 years, with recipes being included in cookbooks as early as the 18th century. There are various versions but it is essentially an almond pastry filled with raspberry or redcurrant jam. As decoration, strips of the pastry are arranged in a grid on top of the cake.

6 Malakofftorte

This rather heavy cake is made of high-calorie ingredients. Unlike most cakes which are baked, the *Malakofftorte* is simply set together with cream and sponge biscuits drenched in rum. In today's health-conscious environment, the traditional buttercream is often substituted with a lower-fat option.

7 Esterhazytorte

Marbled brown-and-white icing is the characteristic element of an *Esterhazytorte*, which is made up of almond sponge layers filled with cream. The very sweet cake is served either in square or wedge-shaped slices.

Esterhazytorte

8 Rehrücken

This chocolate cake is shaped like a saddle of deer, although no one now knows the origin of this. The sponge is usually filled with apricot jam, then glazed with chocolate and studded with almonds, although there are variations.

9 Schwarzwälderkirschtorte

Black Forest Cake is another rich chocolate cake in which layers of sponge cake are sandwiched together with cream and sour cherries. It is then lavishly decorated with crowns of whipped cream, more sour cherries and grated chocolate.

10 Cremeschnitte

This cake consists of two layers of crispy puff pastry filled with a thick layer of vanilla-flavoured whipped cream and topped with sugared icing.

Top 10 Desserts and Pastries

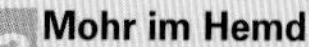

1 Palatschinken
The Austrian pancake is thicker than its French relative and is served with fillings ranging from jam to ice cream, chocolate or curd cheese.

2 Mohr im Hemd
A juicy chocolate-walnut cake served hot with chocolate sauce and whipped cream.

3 Topfengolatsche
These puff pastries are filled with curd cheese and dusted with icing sugar.

4 Zimtschnecke
The rolled puff pastry takes its name from the shape of a snail and is filled with cinnamon and raisins.

5 Marillenknödel
Apricots are hidden inside curd cheese dumplings, covered in breadcrumbs, then roasted in butter.

6 Buchteln
Little yeast cakes filled with plum jam are baked in a large pan so that they stick together. They are usually served with vanilla sauce.

7 Powideltascherl
Little pockets of sweet potato dough are filled with plum jam and simmered in water before being covered with roasted breadcrumbs.

8 Mohnnudeln
The same dough as in *Powideltascherl* is prepared in the shape of noodles and served with poppy seeds.

9 Nusskipferl
A moon-shaped pastry with a walnut or poppy-seed filling.

10 Kaiserschmarrn
Thick pancakes are shredded and sprinkled with raisins and sugar. Often served with a purée of plums.

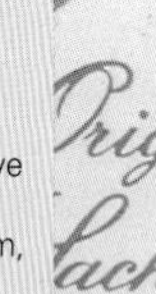

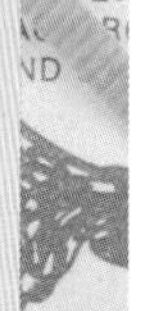

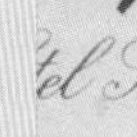

Left **Reinprecht** Right **Kierlinger**

TOP 10 Heurigen

1 Hengl-Haselbrunner

Grinzing *(see p124)* was once a small community of wine-growers but today has one of the highest densities of *Heurigen* in Vienna. The Hengl-Haselbrunner is slightly off the beaten track but offers excellent red and white wines, as well as a buffet menu of regional specialities. Sitting in the courtyard underneath vines in summer is a romantic experience. *Iglaseegasse 10 • U-Bahn U4, U6 • 01 320 33 30 • Dis. access • €€€*

2 Reinprecht

The Reinprecht *Heuriger* is located in a 300-year-old former monastery in Grinzing and has seating in the old vaults as well as on garden terraces. The wines are home-grown, classic *Heurigen* food is served, and you can listen to traditional Viennese *Schrammel* music every evening. *Cobenzlgasse 22 • U-Bahn U4, U6 • 01 320 14 71 0 • Open Jan–Feb: Fri & Sat; Mar–Dec: daily • €€€*

3 Kierlinger

The white wines of this traditional wine tavern are counted among Vienna's best – don't miss the chance to sample a glass of their Chardonnay or Weissburgunder. It is particularly known for its tasty Liptauer spread, made of cheese with paprika, onions, gherkins and various spices. The *Heuriger* also has a large garden, and cultural events take place in the evening all year round. *Kahlenberger Strasse 20 • Train Nussdorf • 01 370 22 64 • No credit cards • Dis. access • €€*

4 Mayer am Pfarrplatz

This historic house, now home to the Mayer *Heuriger*, was once the residence of the composer Ludwig van Beethoven *(see p58)*. He spent the summer of 1817 here when he hoped to find relief for his continually worsening deafness. Today you can soak up the atmosphere at the Mayer *Heuriger* with its excellent food and home-produced wines. Mayer is an acclaimed winery and has won many national and international prizes. Traditional Viennese music is played every evening from 7pm. *Pfarrplatz 2 • U-Bahn U4; Bus 38A • 01 370 33 61 • Dis. access • €€€*

Kahlenberg Heuriger

Heuriger is the Austrian term for a wine tavern that sells home-grown wines by the glass

5 Wieninger

Wieninger is a family business achieving the perfect symbiosis of excellent wines and great food. The wines, particularly Chardonnay grown on the nearby Bisamberg, are among Austria's best and will satisfy any wine connoisseur. The food is exceptionally fine – try the pumpkin seed and cheese spreads. Stammersdorf is one of Vienna's main wine areas, but it is largely frequented by locals, and is therefore less expensive than its more famous sister communities of Grinzing and Nussdorf. *Stammersdorfer Strasse 31 • Bus 30A • 01 292 41 06 • Closed Mon–Wed • No credit cards • Dis. access • €€€ • www.wieninger.at*

WIENINGER
Grüner Veltliner
1991
Kabinett
Weingut Wieninger, 1210 Wien, Stammersdorfer Straße 78
Qualitätswein mit staatlicher Prüf-Nr. K 0005392, 11,0 %vol
ÖSTERREICH trocken e 0,75 l

Wieninger label

6 Fuhrgassl-Huber

This busy *Heuriger* is located on the edge of the Vienna Woods *(see p124)* and, with seating for some 800 people, is one of Vienna's largest wine taverns. There is good food from the traditional buffet – everything from smoked ham and cheese spreads to *Wiener Schnitzel* – and glasses of the most recent vintage. *Neustift am Walde 68 • Bus 41A • 01 440 14 05 • €€€*

7 Sirbu

This *Heuriger*, tucked away on Kahlenberg mountain *(see p124)*, has a stunning setting amid vineyards and trees, and is lovely at night. The usual *Heurigen* dishes and home-grown wines are served. *Kahlenberger Strasse 210 • Train and taxi Nussdorf • 01 320 59 28 • Closed mid-Oct–Apr • €€*

8 Zimmermann

In a friendly family atmosphere, you can enjoy a glass of the new vintages and dishes from the buffet. In summer there is garden seating amid the Neustift vineyards. Zimmermann is a particularly good choice if you plan a *Heurigen* visit with children, as they have a petting zoo with all sorts of small animals. *Mitterwurzergasse 20 • Bus 35A • 01 440 12 07 • Closed Dec–mid-Mar • €€*

9 Christ

This family has been producing wine for 400 years and has been among the top Viennese wine producers several times, winning both national and international awards. The *Heuriger* is a traditional and cosy place, and the garden is a peaceful retreat. Christ serves the traditional *Heurigen* food with seasonal variations, such as asparagus, mushroom or game dishes. *Amtsstrasse 14 • Bus 32A; Tram 31, 32 • Open odd months only • 01 292 51 52 • €€*

10 Zahel

Zahel is an up-and-coming wine producer in Vienna and its excellent red and white wines should not be missed. The *Heuriger* also serves a fine buffet including a changing selection of *à la carte* dishes according to seasonal produce available. The whole place boasts a friendly and cosy atmosphere and in summer seating is also available in the garden. *Maurer Hauptplatz 9 • Bus 60A, 56B; Tram 60 • 01 889 13 18 • Closed Sun • No credit cards • €€*

For a guide to price ranges **See p95**

Left **Café Museum** Right **Café Sperl**

Top 10 Cafés

1 Café Demel

The Demel is Vienna's most refined retreat for cake lovers. Opened in 1786, by the mid-19th century it had become a hotspot for the Viennese upper classes, even providing Empress Sisi with her favourite sweet violet sorbet. *Kohlmarkt 14 • Map M3 • Dis. access*

2 Café Hawelka

The bustling Hawelka, opened in the 1930s, offers old-world charm. The owners often took paintings from artists in exchange for food – as a result the walls are covered with works by Ernst Fuchs, among others. *Dorotheergasse 6 • Map M3 • Dis. access*

3 Café Central

One of the city's best-known cafés, the Central was the meeting place for Vienna's intellectuals at the turn of the 19th century – the poet Peter Altenberg gathered a literary circle and he even had his mail delivered here. Leon Trotsky was also one of the regulars during his Vienna exile prior to World War I. Today the Central serves almost 1,000 cups of coffee a day in its elegant setting *(see p94)*.

Café Central

4 Café Landtmann

Franz Landtmann opened his café in 1873. Sigmund Freud used to have his morning coffee here, as did the artistic director of the Burgtheater, Max Reinhardt. Landtmann bustles with activity day and night, and the four rooms are elegantly decorated with velvet upholstery, crystal light fixtures and mirrors with inlaid wood. *Universitätsring • Map K2 • Dis. access*

5 Café Diglas

Established in 1923, the Diglas has marble tables, wooden chairs and little window booths fitted with red velvet sofas. The newspaper rack and the cakes – slices are served with a small mountain of whipped cream – are obligatory *(see p94)*.

6 Café Bräunerhof

Bräunerhof has a true living-room atmosphere. The furniture is cosy but worn, thanks to a stream of customers dating back to the 1900s. It has always been a literary café – the writers Alfred Polgar and Hugo von Hofmannsthal were regular visitors *(see p94)*.

Regular classical salon music evenings and readings take place at the weekends at Café Bräunerhof – phone ahead for details

7 Café Griensteidl

Founded in 1848, the Café Griensteidl became a meeting place for Vienna's revolutionaries *(see p40)* as well as poets and artists. In summer visitors can sit outside and enjoy the view of the Hofburg opposite.
Michaelerplatz 2 • Map L3 • Dis. access

8 Café Museum

This café was designed by the minimalist architect Adolf Loos in 1899 and reflects his anti-ornamental aesthetic. Remodelled in the 1930s, it has been returned to Loos's original design *(see p114)*.

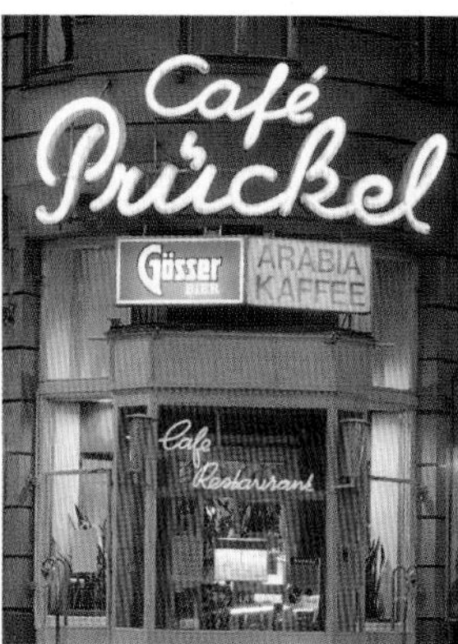

Café Prückel

9 Café Prückel

The Art Nouveau Prückel opened in 1903. The back room, the Golden Hall, is preserved in its original style. *Stubenring 24 • Map Q3 • Dis. access*

10 Café Sperl

This café was built in grand style in 1880 and the regulars (the Sperlianer) have always been artists, singers and musicians from the nearby Theater an der Wien. Concerts take place every Sunday afternoon from September to June *(see p114)*.

Top 10 Types of Coffee

1 Melange
This is a blend of coffee and hot milk, served with foamed milk or whipped cream on the top.

2 Grosser Brauner
A large cup of black coffee is served with a tiny jug of coffee-flavoured cream.

3 Kleiner Brauner
This is the smaller version of the *Grosser Brauner* but also served with cream.

4 Grosser Schwarzer
The drink for real coffee addicts – a very large, strong cup of black coffee with no accompaniment.

5 Kleiner Schwarzer
As the smaller version of the *Grosser Schwarzer*, this is simply just a small cup of black coffee.

6 Verlängerter
This is the "lengthened" variety of a *Brauner*, weakened slightly with hot water and served with milk instead of cream.

7 Kaisermelange
Not to everybody's taste, this is a large black coffee mixed with egg yolk, honey and Cognac.

8 Einspänner
In this version, strong coffee is served in a glass with a crown of whipped cream on top.

9 Fiaker
A large cup of coffee is refined with rum. Named after the city's famous horse-drawn carriages.

10 Eiskaffee
Cold coffee accompanied by vanilla ice cream and whipped cream is served in a tall glass.

Left **Coburg** Right **Fabios**

Top 10 Restaurants

1 Restaurant im Hotel Ambassador

Located on the first floor of the Hotel Ambassador, this gourmet restaurant offers traditional Austrian cuisine with contemporary touches. Seasonal dishes, such as venison and wild boar, feature on the menu, as well as fish and vegetarian fare. The modern dining room is pleasantly light and spacious, overlooking the Neuer Markt. Reservations essential. *Kärntnerstrasse 22 • Map N4 • 01 961 61 0 • Dis. access • €€€€€*

Steirereck

2 Steirereck

With its fabulous service, culinary artistry and opulent location, the Steirereck is arguably the best restaurant in the city. Its menus exhibit stunning flair and have both regional and international influences. Specialities include sturgeon fillets in pepper sauce with crispy olives. In its cellar, around 25,000 bottles of Austrian and international wines wait to be tasted. Reservations are recommended. *Meierei im Stadtpark • Map Q4 • U-Bahn U3, U4; Trams 1, 2 • 01 713 31 68 • Closed Sat–Sun • €€€€€*

3 Plachutta

For the ultimate *Tafelspitz* *(see p70)* you have to go to Plachutta. Authentic, high-quality Viennese cuisine is served, including premium beef from Austrian farmers. There are several Plachuttas all over Vienna and the quality is excellent in all of them. Make sure you book a table, as they all get crowded *(see p95)*.

4 Meinl am Graben

Considered one of the top five restaurants in Austria, the food at Meinl am Graben is simply prepared using top-quality, seasonal ingredients. There is a wide selection of dishes on offer at breakfast, lunchtime and in the evening. This place is also popular for its wine list, which has a choice of over 750 wines. Try to get one of the tables with a wonderful view overlooking Graben. *Graben 19 • Map M3 • 01 532 33 34 • Closed Sun • Dis. access • €€€€€*

5 Fabios

Sleek and stylish, this upmarket, contemporary Italian is popular among Vienna's glitterati. The plush bar and terrace are perfect spots to enjoy cocktails. The array of dishes on offer include octopus marinated in olive oil and parsley; roast guinea fowl with sage on grilled fennel carpaccio; and cold basil soup with deep-fried calamari. *Tuchlauben 6 • Map M3 • 01 532 22 22 • Dis. access • €€€€€*

Do & Co Stephansplatz

6 Do & Co Stephansplatz

If you enjoy a comfortable atmosphere and international cuisine, then this small but fine bistro is the place for you. It is particularly favoured for lunch or early dinner, but many people come just to read the newspapers and enjoy a coffee. In winter, oysters are a speciality *(see p95)*.

7 Kim Kocht

Star Korean chef Sohyi Kim creates inventive, exquisitely presented cuisine, fusing Austrian, Asian and international influences, and using mainly organic produce. Kim will tailor dishes to suit diners' requirements (ask ahead for the menu to be adapted). Advance booking essential. *Merkur Hoher Markt 12 • Map N2 • 01 319 02 42 • Closed Sun • Dis. access • €€€€€*

8 Coburg

Silvio Nickol is among Austria's most celebrated chefs, and specializes in exquisite modern cooking. Savour one of his elaborate set menus with wine accompaniments for an unforgettable gastronomic experience. *Coburgbastei 4 • Map P4 • 01 518 18 80 0 • Dis. access • €€€€€*

9 Palmenhaus

The large Art Nouveau conservatory in the Burggarten is a spectacular setting for a restaurant. Dishes are prepared with high-quality seasonal ingredients and you will always find a great selection of cheeses. There is an impressive wine list. In summer there is an outside cocktail bar with DJs on Fridays, which is open until 2am. *Burggarten/Entrance Albertina • Map M5 • 01 533 10 33 • Dis. access • €€€€*

10 Kervansaray-Hummerbar

One of Vienna's most famous seafood restaurants, the first-floor Hummerbar serves excellent lobster, oysters and caviar. The restaurant Kervansaray on the ground floor specializes in Turkish-influenced meat and fish dishes and probably has Vienna's most beautiful *meze* buffet. *Mahlerstrasse 9 • Map N5 • 01 512 88 43 • Closed Sun • Dis. access • No vegetarian options • €€€€€*

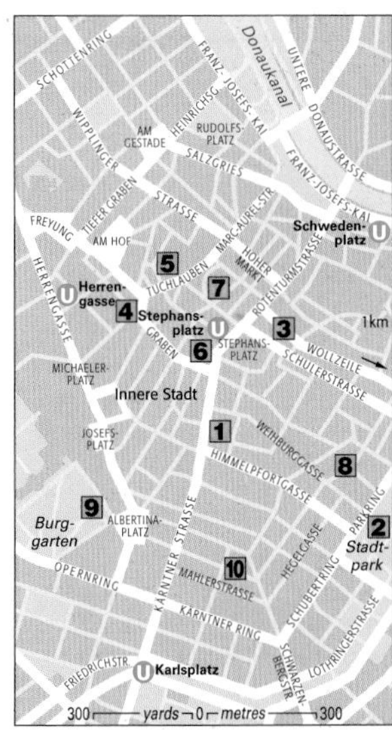

For a guide to restaurant price ranges **See p95**

Left **Wiener Festwochen** Right **Painted Easter eggs**

TOP 10 Festivals

1 Ball Season

Viennese life revolves around the waltz – at least during *Fasching*, the period between Christmas and Lent, when the social calendar is packed with evenings of ballroom dancing. Balls in the Hofburg Palace are the most splendid, but you will find dances every evening in many of Vienna's hotels, concert halls and once a year in the State Opera House *(see pp30–31)*.

2 Wiener Festwochen

The annual theatre festival is held in May and June, when productions by theatre and dance companies are staged at venues such as the Museumsquartier, the Ronacher and Theater an der Wien *(see pp28–9 & 61)*.

3 Jazzfest

Homes of classical music such as the State Opera and the Konzerthaus turn into jazz venues during Vienna's annual Jazzfest. From mid-June until early July, world-famous jazz musicians perform all over Vienna.

4 Christmas Markets

In the weeks before Christmas you will find numerous markets across Vienna's squares and pedestrianized zones. The stalls sell mainly small gifts and Christmas decorations, as well as punch and hot spiced wine to warm you on cold winter evenings.

5 Musikfilmfest

Every July and August the square in front of Vienna's Town Hall turns into a bustling hub for music lovers. Every evening crowds flock to watch concerts and opera and operetta performances broadcast on a huge video screen. Just as popular are the food stalls where Mexican, Japanese, Greek and Austrian specialities can all be found.

6 ImPulsTanz

Also in July and August, Vienna turns into the capital of dance when the international dance festival takes place at various theatres.

7 Wien Modern

Founded by Claudio Abbado in 1988, Wien Modern is one of Europe's few genuinely successful festivals for post-1945 and contemporary "classical" music. The emphasis is on the avant-garde, and the concerts, principally at the Konzerthaus, play to large and enthusiastic audiences.

Christmas Market stall

Musikfilmfest

8 Viennale

The Viennale, the city's international film festival, takes place in October every year. Screenings are held in cinemas in the historic centre of the city. These include many special films that would probably not make it to Vienna's mainstream cinemas in other circumstances. Accompanying debates and events take place in a tent in Stadtpark.

9 Easter Markets

Austria's Easter tradition is to decorate branches of pussy willow with painted eggshells hung on a string. Easter Egg Markets, with eggs in all colours and shades, are also held on squares and in front of churches.

10 Oper Klosterneuburg

In July, Oper Klosterneuburg stages glamorous performances of opera classics in the courtyard of Klosterneuburg abbey, the palatial religious foundation that dominates the town of the same name just north of Vienna *(see p128)*. There are also behind-the-scenes workshops for children.

Top 10 Religious Festivals

1 Epiphany

The last day of the Christmas holidays. Children dress as the Three Wise Men and knock on doors to bring news of Christ's birth. *6 Jan*

2 Easter

The feast of joy as Christ is resurrected from the dead is celebrated with fires and light processions. *Mar/Apr*

3 Christ's Ascension

Celebrated on the nearest Thursday 40 days after Easter to mark the day Christ ascended to heaven.

4 Pentecost

Celebrates the Holy Ghost being sent to unite the world's peoples 50 days after Easter.

5 Corpus Christi

Processions are held in every parish and a monstrance decorated with flowers is carried from altar to altar.

6 Mary's Ascension

This day commemorates the Virgin Mary's ascension to heaven. *15 Aug*

7 All Saints' Day

Austrians visit the graves of their beloved to light candles and lay wreaths. *1 Nov*

8 Mary's Conception

On this day, St Anne conceived a daughter, the Virgin Mary. *8 Dec*

9 Christmas Eve

The most important day of the celebrations, as families gather around the Christmas tree and open presents. *24 Dec*

10 Christmas Day

A holy day when people attend church and visit their families. Christmas dinner is traditionally carp or goose. *25 Dec*

Following pages: **Parliament building**

AROUND TOWN

Left **Looshaus** Right **Postsparkasse**

Central Vienna

WITH COBBLED STREETS, NARROW ALLEYS, QUIET SQUARES *and historic buildings, Vienna's atmospheric heart is brimming with famous landmarks and reminders of Roman and Habsburg rule, yet it also hosts the* crème de la crème *of shops, restaurants and cafés. Although the inner city is popular with visitors, nowhere else will you find so many elegant locals proudly promenading as you will along the Kärntner Strasse, Graben and Kohlmarkt – indeed, most of the central area is now pedestrianized.*

Sights

1. Stephansdom
2. Hofburg Palace
3. Burgtheater
4. Postsparkasse
5. Misrachi-Haus
6. Ruprechtskirche
7. Albertina
8. Looshaus
9. Anker Uhr
10. Donnerbrunnen

Altar, Stephansdom

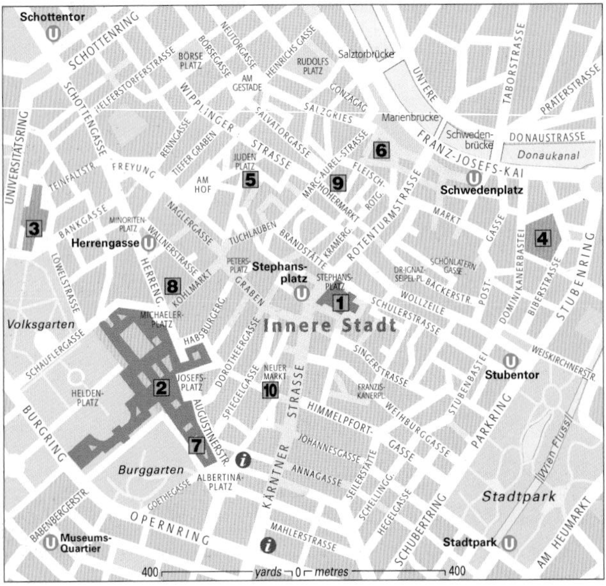

1 Stephansdom

At the geographical epicentre of the city, the spectacular Gothic Stephansdom cathedral dominates the skyline with its many towers and its 137-m (450-ft) spire *(see pp8–11)*.

2 Hofburg Palace

The former imperial palace may have relinquished its regal position after Austria became a republic in 1918, but the elegance of days gone by is still tangible in its sumptuous state apartments, landscaped gardens and various architectural styles *(see pp12–17)*.

3 Burgtheater

The Burg, as the theatre is affectionately called by the Viennese, was among the first theatres to be built in the German-speaking world. Gottfried Semper and Carl von Hasenauer designed this spectacular building with its Renaissance façade over a period of 14 years (1874–88). On its completion, the Court Theatre, founded in 1776, moved into the new building on the Ringstrasse. A grand staircase with frescoes by Gustav Klimt and his brother Ernst leads from the foyer to the auditorium *(see p56)*. Emperor Franz Joseph awarded them a Golden Cross of Merit for their work. *Universitätsring 2 • Map K2 • Guided tours 3pm daily (tel. 01 514 44 41 40) • Adm*

4 Postsparkasse

In the unlikely setting of the Postsparkasse building (the post office savings bank) Otto Wagner *(see p109)* implemented all his principles, combining functionalism within an appealing design. The square six-storey building, constructed in two stages between 1904 and 1912, has a plain façade of marble and granite. The stone panels are fixed to the external walls with metal rivets, which led to the building's nickname "a box of nails" among locals. The solid-looking exterior, however, is contrasted by the light interior, covered with a glazed vault. *Georg-Coch-Platz 2 • Map Q3 • Open 8am–3pm Mon–Wed & Fri, 8am–5:30pm Thu • Free*

Burgtheater

5 Misrachi-Haus

During the construction of a Holocaust memorial by London artist Rachel Whiteread on Judenplatz in 2000, the remains of a medieval synagogue were discovered. Once the centre of a flourishing Jewish community, the synagogue was destroyed in 1420 and its bricks used for building the old university. The excavation site is open to the public and a small museum is dedicated to the life, work and religion of the city's medieval Jewish community. You can also take a virtual stroll around the 15th-century Jewish quarter. *Judenplatz 8 • Map M2 • Open 10am–6pm Sun–Thu, 10am–2pm Fri • Adm • www.jmw.at*

6 Ruprechtskirche

This church boasts the title of Vienna's oldest place of worship, built in the 9th century after the fall of Vindobona *(see p40)* as part of the settlements within the Roman city walls. The stone building was the city's main church until the end of the 12th century, when the Stephansdom became Vienna's most important centre of worship. Both east windows date back to the 13th century and have survived the ages untouched as Vienna's oldest works of stained glass. *Ruprechtsplatz • Map N2 • Open 10am–noon & 3–5pm Mon–Fri • Free*

Jewish Vienna

The Jewish Quarter centres around the cobbled streets and squares in the vicinity of the "city temple" synagogue, built in 1825 in Seitenstettengasse. But today the picturesque district with its pretty houses is more famous for its bars and restaurants than for the Jewish community; that is now based in the Karmeliter quarter of the 2nd district.

Sculpture, Albertina

7 Albertina

One of the world's largest and most valuable collections of graphic art is gathered in the Albertina palace, named after its founder, Duke Albert of Sachsen-Teschen (1738–1822). Temporary exhibitions feature loaned paintings and photographs, as well as prints and drawings from the Albertina itself. *Albertinaplatz 1 • Map M5 • U-Bahn Karlsplatz, Stephansplatz • Open 10am–6pm daily (until 9pm Wed) • Adm (free for under 19s) • www.albertina.at*

8 Looshaus

No other building triggered so much controversy as the Looshaus, completed in 1911. Emperor Franz Joseph thought the functional building ruined the square's look and had the curtains closed at his Hofburg palace to avoid looking at it. Four floors are covered in green marble but the building's plain upper floors caused uproar. Today it is home to a bank. *Michaelerplatz 3 • Map L3 • Open 8am–3pm Mon–Wed & Fri, 8am–5:30pm Thu • Dis. access • Free*

If you are in Vienna during advent, you can listen to Christmas carols played by the Anker Uhr's Glockenspiel at 5pm and 6pm

9 Anker Uhr

The Anker Uhr clock spans two wings of an insurance company building and was installed between 1911 and 1917 by Franz von Matsch. Every day 12 pairs of figures, each symbolizing a period in Vienna's history, step forward on the hour. The Roman Emperor Marcus Aurelius begins, followed by Duke Leopold VI, Maria Theresa and Joseph Haydn, among others. At noon, all 12 figures parade across the bridge.
Hoher Markt 10/11 • Map N2 • Free

Anker Uhr

10 Donnerbrunnen

The centrepiece of the Neuer Markt is Georg Raphael Donner's fountain (1737–9) with an allegory of Providentia, the divine providence, accompanied by four cherubs towering over a pool. They are surrounded by four figures representing the rivers Traun, Enns, March and Ybbs. Regarded improper, the naked statues were removed during Maria Theresa's reign but they were replaced with replicas in the 19th century. The originals are now in the Lower Belvedere *(see p53)*. *Neuer Markt • Map M4*

A Day's Stroll in Central Vienna

Morning

Begin the day at the **Stephansdom** *(see pp8–11)* to catch the morning sun beaming through the medieval windows, and stroll around the cathedral's Gothic features. It is worth climbing the South Tower or taking the elevator up the North Tower for stunning views over the rooftops. For a mid-morning break, head to the far end of the square and enjoy a cup of tea in **Haas & Haas** *(see p94)*.

Wander the narrow streets around the cathedral but arrive on Hoher Markt at noon to watch the historic figures of the **Anker Uhr** march by.

There are many places to have lunch, but on a sunny day pick **Do & Co** *(see p95)* with its terrace overlooking Stephansplatz.

Afternoon

Spend the early afternoon exploring Graben and Kohlmarkt, with their antiques shops and galleries, until you reach the **Hofburg Palace** *(see pp12–17)*. With its various collections, select those that interest you most, but don't miss the state apartments where Emperor Franz Joseph lived.

Leave the palace through the Michaeler Gate, pass the **Looshaus**, then treat yourself to a coffee and a piece of Sachertorte at the refined **Café Demel** *(see p76)*.

Finally, take tram No. 1 from Karlsplatz to Schwedenplatz to admire the floodlit buildings by night.

Following pages: **Grand staircase, Burgtheater**

Left **Kirche am Hof** Right **Pestsäule**

TOP 10 Best of the Rest

1 Akademie der Wissenschaften

This Rococo building (1755) was formerly the site of Vienna University. The Academy of Sciences hall staged the premiere of Joseph Haydn's *The Creation* in 1808. *Dr-Ignaz-Seipel-Platz • Map P3 • Open 9am–5pm Mon–Fri • Adm*

2 Franziskanerplatz

This charming square is home to the Franciscan church *(see p48)*, picturesque old houses and the Moses fountain (1798). *Franziskanerplatz • Map N4*

3 Peterskirche

A Baroque church with a monumental high altar and frescoes by Michael Rottmayr. *Petersplatz • Map M3*

4 Altes Rathaus

The Habsburgs confiscated this palace in 1316 from Otto von Haymo, who had conspired against them. It functioned as the town hall until 1883. *Wipplingerstrasse 8 • Map N2 • Closed to the public*

5 Kirche am Hof

Emperor Ferdinand III's widow had this monumental church built in 1662. It is more reminiscent of a palace than a place of worship. *Am Hof 7 • Map M2*

6 Pestsäule

After a plague epidemic that killed more than 100,000 came to an end in 1679, Emperor Leopold I had this Baroque monument installed, dedicating it to the Holy Trinity. *Graben • Map M3*

7 Börse

Once the home of the Vienna Stock Exchange, this Theophil von Hansen Classicist building is now used by the government. *Schottenring 16 • Map L1*

8 Kapuzinerkirche

Built in 1618, the simple design of this church is in line with the Capuchin order's doctrine. Emperor Matthias (1557–1619) established a crypt for the Habsburgs here *(see p62)*. *Neuer Markt • Map M4*

9 Minoritenkirche

When Duke Leopold VI returned safely from a crusade in 1219, he built a church on this site. Its medieval character is still visible. *Minoritenplatz 2 • Map L3*

10 Heiligenkreuzerhof

Founded in the Middle Ages as a monastery, today the building hosts the city's arts college. *Schönlaterngasse • Map P3*

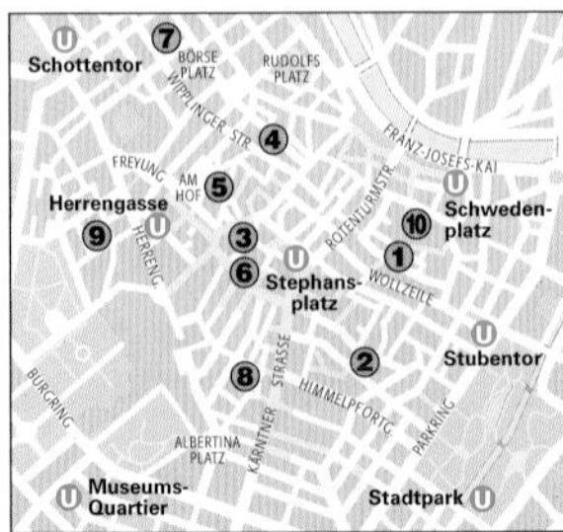

Left **American Bar** Right **Planter's Club**

TOP 10 Clubs and Bars

1 American Bar
The small bar in a simple but sophisticated Adolf Loos design is one of the most beautiful nightspots in town. It also serves delectable cocktails. *Kärntner Strasse 10 • Map N4*

2 Planter's Club
In the Colonial-style bar with luxurious furniture and teak wood panelling, mouthwatering cocktails are served. You can also choose from more than 300 whiskies and 90 rums. *Zelinkagasse 4 • Map C4*

3 Bermuda Bräu
This bustling pub, in an area known as the Bermuda Triangle, is renowned for its draught beer served in clay jugs, as well as its variety of bottled beers. There is a dance floor in the basement. *Rabensteig 6 • Map P2*

4 Palmenhaus
This renovated Imperial greenhouse hosts a stylish restaurant and bar offering fine Austrian wines and occasional live DJ nights. The real star, however, is the beautiful glass building. *Burggarten/Goethegasse • Map M5*

5 Volksgarten
The Volksgarten is one of the city's most established party zones, with a varied mix of music – soul, funk, hip-hop and house. There's a fabulous garden in summer. *Burgring 1 • Map K4*

6 Onyx Bar
Vienna's in-crowd gathers in this bar with its magnificent view of the Stephansdom *(see pp8–11)*. Snacks, cocktails and groovy background music are on offer. *Haas-Haus, Stephansplatz 12, 7th floor • Map N3*

7 Havana Club
Great Cuban atmosphere for salsa fanatics and lashings of rum attracts a crowd of locals and expats. Each day has its own motto. There are also dance instructors and guest DJs. *Mahlerstrasse 11 • Map N6*

8 Skybar
Very popular among the well-to-do young Viennese, this trendy place has a great atmosphere with a view over Vienna's rooftops. Good wines and cocktails. *Kärntner Strasse 19 • Map N4*

9 Ma Pitom
This cosy beer hall not only offers a large variety of national and international beers but also live music and cultural events. Toys, books and special facilities for kids are also available. *Seitenstettengasse 5 • Map N2*

10 Roter Engel
Music is the speciality of this bar, with Viennese artists playing everything from rock to pop, funk and soul, every Monday to Thursday. *Rabensteig 5 • Map P2*

Left **Central Vienna shop signs** Centre **Loden coat** Right **Shakespeare & Co**

Top 10 Specialist Shops

1 Haas & Haas
This shop offers more than 200 assorted fruit teas, black teas, herbal teas and many tea accessories. The marzipan confectionery and chocolates are divine. *Stephansplatz 4 • Map N3*

2 Xocolat
Everything in this little shop revolves around chocolate, with more than 120 varieties from all over the world, as well as books on the subject. *Freyung 2, in the Palais Ferstel • Map L2*

3 Doblinger
This music publishing house, which has been in business for 125 years, has every music sheet a musician can dream of. Be it classical or contemporary music, Doblinger has it. *Dorotheergasse 10 • Map M4*

4 Mayr & Fessler
The best address for top-of-the-range fountain pens, as well as diaries and organizers. It has a wide range of Italian writing and wrapping paper as well as notebooks and accessories. *Kärntner Strasse 37 • Map N4*

5 Gmundner Ceramics
Austrian hand-painted pottery is produced at Gmunden in Upper Austria. The traditional green-on-white decoration looks sloshed-on, but perfect. Wide range of wares and patterns just outside the Ring behind Parliament. *Stadiongasse 7 • Map D2*

6 Shakespeare & Co
A tiny bookshop with a lot of character and the best place to go for contemporary English literature. Good travel and poetry section. *Sterngasse 2 • Map N2*

7 Knize
Custom-made clothing has been the focus of this elegant establishment for nearly 150 years. The shop itself is internationally admired, as Adolf Loos transformed it into a masterpiece in 1910. *Graben 13 • Map M3*

8 Loden Plankl
This old family business offers traditional Austrian clothing ranging from Loden coats and jackets to beautiful Dirndl dresses and Lederhosen (leather trousers). It also stocks modern variations of traditional garments. *Michaelerplatz 6 • Map L3*

9 Meinl am Graben
One of the best delicatessens in town, with a great selection of exquisite chocolates, dessert wines and coffees. Have a look in the beautifully decorated windows. *Am Graben 19 • Map M3*

10 Augarten Flagship Store
The porcelain at the city outlet of Vienna's historic factory ranges from exquisite tableware to Wiener Werkstätte designs and modern *objets d'art*. *Spiegelgasse 3 • Map M4*

For tips on shopping in Vienna **See p140**

Left **Wiener Interieur** Right **Alte Kunst und Militaria**

Galleries and Antiques Shops

1 Dorotheum Auction House

Vienna is well-known for its antiques, and Dorotheergasse is one of the main areas to head for if this is your interest. At the city's main auction house, in operation since 1907, you can buy everything from antique furniture to jewellery and paintings. Prices can be rather steep, but it's a fascinating place to browse around if you can't afford to buy. *Dorotheergasse 17 • Map M4 • www.dorotheum.at*

2 Wiener Interieur

Situated among the many galleries and antiques shops in Dorotheergasse, Wiener Interieur has beautiful jewellery from the beginning of the 20th century up to the 1960s. A gem-lover's paradise. *Dorotheergasse 14 • Map M4*

3 Maria Griemann

Here you can find signs and posters that comprised some of the first-ever advertisements in Austria and around the world, as well as antique toys and striking glassware. *Spiegelgasse 14 • Map M4*

4 Galerie Ambiente

Beautiful and innovative furniture from Viennese designers and manufacturers, such as Josef Hoffmann and Thonet, is sold at Ambiente. They can also arrange shipping to get your goods home. *Lugeck 1 • Map N3 • www.ambientegalerieambiente.at*

5 Antiquariat Inlibris Gilhofer Nfg.

Scientific books, early prints and Austrian memorabilia are some of the specialities of this antiquarian bookshop. *Rathausstrasse 19 • Map J3 • www.inlibris.at*

6 Alte Kunst und Militaria

Old uniforms from the imperial age and military medals are on display here. *Plankengasse 7 • Map M4 • www.militaria-koeck.at*

7 Galerie Hofstätter

This gallery organizes several major exhibitions a year of Austrian postwar and contemporary artists. *Bräunerstrasse 7 • Map M4 • www.galerie-hofstaetter.com*

8 Galerie Hilger

Early 20th-century art and contemporary Austrian and international artists are shown in nine exhibitions a year here. *Dorotheergasse 5 • Map M4 • www.hilger.at*

9 Galerie Charim

This gallery in the former Palais Gatterburg specializes in Austrian art, such as new media and object art, as well as photography. *Dorotheergasse 12 • Map M4 • www.charimgalerie.at*

10 Antiquitäten Sonja Reisch

Silver and tableware, as well as glass and decorative objects from the Biedermeier era, can be found at this very well-run shop. *Bräunerstrasse 10 • Map M3 • www.antiquitaeten-reisch.com*

Left **Café Frauenhuber** Right **Kleines Café**

TOP 10 Cafés and Tearooms

1 Kleines Café
The café is tiny, as its name suggests, with only a few tables, but it has a great atmosphere. In summer there is seating outside on beautiful Franziskanerplatz. *Franziskanerplatz 3 • Map N4*

2 Trzesniewski
This Vienna institution is famous for its delicious selection of small, open sandwiches. Complete your order with the traditional accompaniment of a *Pfiff* (beer). *Dorotheergasse 1 • Map M3*

3 Café Diglas
A very charming, small traditional café with stuccoed walls, Diglas sells mouth-watering cakes and you can even watch how apple strudel, Sachertorte and the like are made in the historic bakery. *Fleischmarkt 16 • Map P2*

4 Haas & Haas Teehaus
Just behind the Stephansdom, located in an old convent, this stylish tearoom serves 12 different kinds of delicious breakfasts, as well as afternoon tea and light lunches. For a treat, try the Haas & Haas "special breakfast". *Stephansplatz 4 • Map N3*

5 Café Frauenhuber
One of the city's oldest and most beautiful cafés, with cosy red sofas and marble tables. A wide variety of cakes and snacks are available. *Himmelpfortgasse 6 • Map N4*

6 Café Central
Situated in the historic Palais Ferstel, this café was the meeting point for the city's intellectuals in the late 19th and early 20th centuries. Live piano music daily *(see p76)*. *Herrengasse 14 • Map L2*

7 Café Bräunerhof
A literary café that offers an extensive range of coffees, excellent cakes and the international papers. Piano music at weekends *(see p76)*. *Stallburggasse 2 • Map M4*

8 Café Mozart
Shortly after Mozart's death in 1791, this café was established in his name. Today it is a classic Viennese café and restaurant, offering not only snacks but also main courses. *Albertinaplatz 2 • Map M5*

9 Café Tirolerhof
This traditional Viennese café offers a variety of tasty cakes, among them excellent *Apfelstrudel*. You can read a range of international daily papers while sipping your coffee. *Führichgasse 8 • Map M5*

10 Demmers Teehaus
The tearoom is part of a shop with more than 300 specialist teas. There are fine fruit, black and green teas, as well as little snacks, such as scones, cakes and sandwiches. *Mölker Bastei 5 • Map K2*

Price Categories

For a three-course meal for one with half a bottle of wine (or equivalent meal), taxes and extra charges.		
	€	under €25
	€€	€25–€35
	€€€	€35–€55
	€€€€	€55–€70
	€€€€€	over €70

Above **Augustiner-Keller**

Top 10 Traditional Viennese Restaurants

1 Figlmüller

This traditional Viennese eatery is famous for its large *Schnitzel* that literally overlap the plates. *Wollzeile 5 • Map N3 • 01 512 17 60 • Dis. access • €€€*

2 Zum weissen Rauchfangkehrer

Once the place where Vienna's chimney-sweepers met, this restaurant with cosy atmosphere serves Viennese cuisine, such as *Tafelspitz* *(see p70)*. Extensive wine list. *Weihburggasse 4 • Map N4 • 01 512 3417 • €€€€*

3 Do & Co Stephansplatz

This very stylish restaurant offers a selection of the best dishes from around the world, ranging from classic Viennese cuisine to sushi and Thai food. Overlooks Stephansdom. *Stephansplatz 12 • Map N3 • 01 535 3969 • Dis. access • €€€€€*

4 Österreicher im MAK

This buzzy restaurant in the Museum for Applied Arts serves up classic Viennese food with a contemporary twist. Reasonable prices and a great selection of Austrian wines by the glass make this a popular choice. *Stubenring 5 • Map Q3 • 01 714 0121 • €€€*

5 Plachutta

Plachutta is the beef specialist in town. Don't miss the *Tafelspitz* with roasted potatoes *(see p78)*. *Wollzeile 38 • Map N3 • 01 512 1577 • €€€€*

6 Weibels Wirsthaus

Specializing in Viennese classics, this is also one of the best places to sample the country's viniculture. *Kumpfgasse 2 • Map P4 • 01 512 3986 • Dis. access • €€€*

7 Zum Schwarzen Kameel

Premium Viennese cuisine in a stunning Art Nouveau setting. *Bognergasse 5 • Map M3 • 01 533 8125 • €€€€€*

8 Hopferl

Tasty meals such as medallion of pork in dark beer sauce are on offer here. *Naglergasse 13 • Map M3 • 01 533 2641 • €€*

9 Augustiner-Keller

Located in a cellar underneath the Albertina, with a menu of Viennese specialities. Live music from 6:30pm. *Augustinerstrasse 1 • Map M5 • 01 533 1026 • €€*

10 Stadtbeisl Inigo

Viennese and international cuisine. Wine list changes every other month. *Bäckerstrasse 18 • Map P3 • 01 512 7451 • Dis. access • €€*

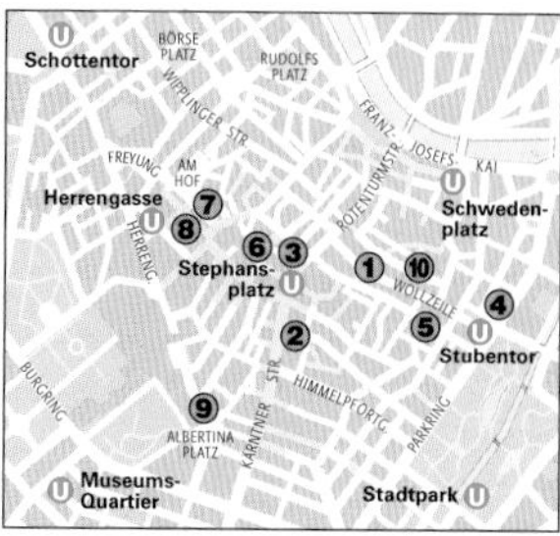

Note: *Unless otherwise stated, all restaurants accept credit cards and serve vegetarian meals*

Left **Sigmund Freud Museum** Right **Vienna University**

Schottenring and Alsergrund

A LARGE PART OF THE ALSERGRUND DISTRICT *is inhabited by medical institutions, including the huge twin-towered AKH general hospital and the Vienna medical school – even the student bars here are built on the site of a former hospital. This is perhaps not surprising in the area where the psychoanalyst Sigmund Freud lived and worked in the early 20th century. The skyline is also dominated by the Votivkirche, which looks out across a park towards the city centre.*

Sights

1. **Votivkirche**
2. **Vienna University**
3. **Sigmund Freud Museum**
4. **Altes Allgemeines Krankenhaus**
5. **Strudlhofstiege**
6. **Rossauer Kaserne**
7. **Palais Liechtenstein**
8. **Josephinum**
9. **Schubert's House of Birth**
10. **Servitenkirche**

Statues, Votivkirche

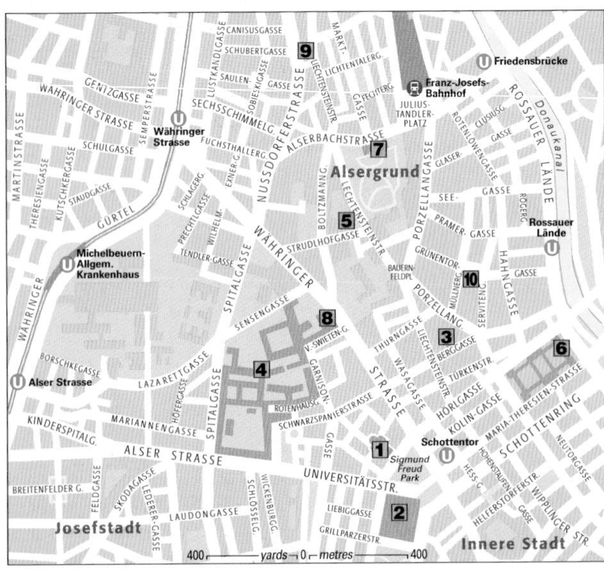

1 Votivkirche

This sandstone church with its ornate façade is part of the grand Ringstrasse. After Franz Joseph had survived a knife attack by the Hungarian tailor Johann Libenyi in 1853, his brother Maximilian raised funds to build this church in gratitude. Many of the building's side chapels are dedicated to military heroes, among them Niklaus von Salm, who commanded the troops in the Turkish Siege of 1529. There are services in English on Sundays *(see p48)*. *Rooseveltplatz • Map C3 • Open 9am–1pm & 4–6:30pm Tue–Sat, 9am–1pm Sun • Dis. access • Free*

2 Vienna University

Vienna University was founded by Duke Rudolf IV in 1365 and today has around 60,000 students. The present building was constructed in Italian Renaissance style on a former army parade ground following plans by Heinrich Ferstel, and opened in 1884. From the entrance hall with marble columns, grand staircases lead to the lecture theatres and the library. The arcaded courtyard is lined with busts of distinguished professors and the university's eight Nobel Prize winners. The ceremony hall is decorated with frescoes by Gustav Klimt (1895) depicting the various faculties. *Universitätsring 1 • Map K1 • Open Mon–Sat • Free*

3 Sigmund Freud Museum

The founder of psychoanalysis *(see p98)* lived in Vienna from 1891 until 1938, when he fled from the National Socialists to London. In his spacious apartment in Berggasse, now a museum, he wrote many famous works and case histories such as *The Interpretation of Dreams*.

Votivkirche

His former consulting rooms and office have been turned into exhibition rooms displaying his original furniture. There is also a library and a lecture hall. *Berggasse 19 • Map B3 • Open 9am–5pm daily • Adm • www.freud-museum.at*

4 Altes Allgemeines Krankenhaus

This huge hospital complex with 11 courtyards is an oasis of tranquillity. At end of the 18th century Emperor Joseph II converted an existing house for the poor into a general hospital, which included a "birth house", a "foundling house" and a "mad house" – today this houses a pathological museum *(see p47)*. The complex was still used as a hospital up to the early 1980s but was then given to Vienna University and adapted for the the campus's arts departments. *Spitalgasse 2 • Map B2 • Open daily • Dis. access • Free*

5 Strudlhofstiege

This striking Art Nouveau double staircase which winds its way down from Strudlhofgasse to Liechtensteinstrasse was designed by Theodor Jäger in 1910. Two fountains, chandeliers and various ramps create a graceful impression. It became famous in 1951, when the Austrian writer Heimito von Doderer published a novel named after the stairway.
Strudlhofgasse/Liechtensteinstrasse • Map B3

6 Rossauer Kaserne

These huge barracks dominating the river bank were created to protect Vienna from attacks from outside the city as well as revolt from within, after the revolutions that took place across Europe in 1848. Together with two other military camps, the Rossauer base formed a strategic triangle. Work on the barracks, which were created in Windsor style, started in 1864 and was completed six years later. The barracks became the headquarters of the Vienna police after World War II. *Schlickplatz 6 • Map B4 • Closed to the public*

Sigmund Freud

In his study of the unconscious mind, Sigmund Freud (1856–1939) divided the human psyche into three different levels (id, ego and superego) that, whenever they are unbalanced, are expressed in dreams, Freudian slips or mental disorder. But Dr Freud observed in his patients that these mental problems tended to disappear after forgotten material, mainly rooted in childhood, was made conscious. His ideas were the foundation of modern-day psychoanalysis.

Fresco, Palais Liechtenstein

7 Palais Liechtenstein

Constructed as the summer residence for the Liechtenstein family at the end of the 17th century, the Palais Liechtenstein is Vienna's premier home of Baroque art. This magnificent private collection includes works by many important artists, such as Raphael, the Brueghels, Rubens, Van Dyck and Rembrandt. There are several temporary exhibitions. The well-maintained gardens are also open to the public *(see p50)*.
Fürstengasse 1 • Map A3 • Open for groups by appt only (tel. 01 319 57 67 252) • Adm • www.liechtensteinmuseum.at

8 Josephinum

Founded by Emperor Joseph II in 1785 as a medical academy, the Josephinum initially trained military doctors, and later general practitioners. Today these buildings host the Institute for the History of Medicine and an anatomical museum *(see p47)*. *Währinger Strasse 25 • Map B3 • Open 10am–6pm Fri & Sat • Adm*

9 Schubert's House of Birth

Franz Schubert was born in the kitchen of this little first-floor apartment, now a museum, on 31 January 1797 and spent the first four years of his life in the property, known locally as "House of the Red Crab". The apartment, which is entered via a wooden balcony, had only one small room facing the street. The museum presents information on the composer's life *(see p58)* as well as various portraits by Schubert's contemporaries. The highlight of the exhibition is Schubert's famous spectacles. *Nussdorfer Strasse 54 • Map A2 • Open 10am–1pm & 2–6pm Tue–Sun & public hols; closed 1 Jan, 1 May & 25 Dec • Adm*

10 Servitenkirche

Although this charming church is slightly off the beaten track, it is well worth a visit. The early Baroque church and an adjoining monastery were built in 1651 by the Servite convent. The interior is decorated with stucco ornaments and frescoes, but an interesting detail is the 13th-century crucifix to the right of the high altar. Originally the "cross of gallows", it stood at the public execution place on Schlickplatz.
Servitengasse 9 • Map B3 • Open 9am–10pm daily • Free

Pietà detail, Servitenkirche

A Day in Vienna's Student District

Morning

Start your day at **Vienna University** *(see p97)*, exploring the marble entrance hall and the courtyard. Then head towards the **Votivkirche** *(see p97)*, passing through **Sigmund Freud Park** *(see p53)*.

Walk up Alser Strasse until you reach the former General Hospital. For a break, choose one of the many pubs in the large first courtyard, amid crowds of students.

Head to courtyard 13, where the **Pathologisch-Anatomisches Museum** *(see p47)* is situated. Cut your way to Strudlhofgasse and stride down **Strudlhofstiege**, where you can already spot **Palais Liechtenstein**. In Porzellangasse you will find several places for a hearty lunch.

Afternoon

On your way to the **Sigmund Freud Museum** *(see p97)*, pass by **Servitenkirche** and get a glimpse of the Baroque interior. Give yourself enough time to have a look around Dr Freud's apartment and consulting rooms. For a break and a cup of coffee, **Café Berg** *(see p100)* just across the road is a great place to rest your feet. Then visit the collection of 18th-century anatomical wax models in the **Josephinum**.

You can round the day off with a visit to Votiv Kino, an arts cinema that shows independent films in their original language on Währinger Strasse 12 *(tel. 317 35 71)*.

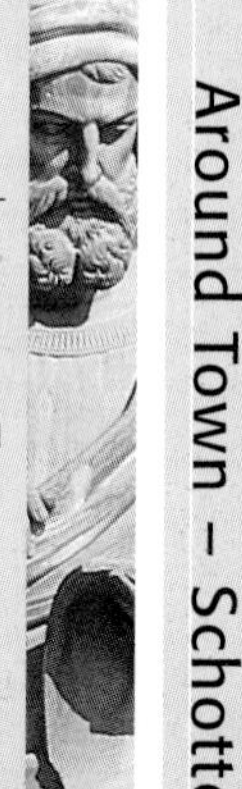

Left **Zwillingsgwölb** Right **Cafeteria Maximilian**

TOP 10 Student Hangouts

1 Stiegl's Alte Ambulanz
Excellent draught and bottled beer and hearty snacks, such as huge toasted sandwiches. There's seating underneath the large chestnut trees in summer. Relaxing atmosphere. *University Campus, Alser Strasse 4 • Map C2*

2 Café Berg
A trendy hangout with cosy rattan seating and an adjoining bookshop. Popular with Vienna's gay community. *Berggasse 8 • Map C3*

3 Cafeteria Maximilian
Located just a stone's throw from Vienna University, it is not surprising that this lively café is usually crowded with students. Warming cups of tea, coffee and hot chocolate, as well as light snacks such as toasted sandwiches, are on offer. *Universitätsstrasse 2 • Map K1*

4 Statt-Beisl WUK
This former 19th-century locomotive factory has been cleverly converted into a cultural centre and operates a café and restaurant. *Währinger Strasse 59 • Map B2*

5 Zwillingsgwölb
Just behind the university is Zwillingsgwölb (twin vaults) with a pleasant café-type restaurant on the ground floor and an atmospheric pub in the cellar. *Universitätsstrasse 5 • Map K1*

6 Café Votiv
The charming café within the Votiv cinema is popular with students as well as, of course, cinema-goers before and after film screenings. *Währinger Strasse 12 • Map C3*

7 Gangl
Beer on tap, toasted sandwiches and a cosy atmosphere, as well as seating outside in summer, attracts a loyal crowd of students. Generally crowded. *University Campus, Alser Strasse 4 • Map C2*

8 Sigmund Freud Park
On a sunny day the lawns of Sigmund Freud Park, just opposite the university buildings, are inhabited by crowds of students studying, picnicking, sunbathing and debating the latest issues. *Map K1*

9 Café Stein
This hotspot has seating inside and out, and offers a good view of the Votivkirche *(see p97)*. A great choice for a traditional breakfast. It also hosts various cultural events. *Währinger Strasse 6–8 • Map C3*

10 Charlie P's
One of the many Irish pubs dotted around the city, Charlie P's has a particularly lively atmosphere. An essential part of the traditional menu is fish and chips and a pint of Guinness. *Währinger Strasse 3 • Map C3*

Price Categories

For a three-course meal for one with half a bottle of wine (or equivalent meal), taxes and extra charges.

€	under €25
€€	€25–€35
€€€	€35–€55
€€€€	€55–€70
€€€€€	over €70

Above **Universitätsbräuhaus**

Top 10 Places to Eat

1 Roth
This restaurant with red seating and red panelling on the walls offers a great selection of Austrian dishes and wines. *Währinger Strasse 1 • Map C3 • 01 402 7995 • €€€€*

2 Universitätsbräuhaus
Enjoy simple but tasty dishes in the pharmacy of the former 18th-century hospital, now a restaurant. *University Campus, Alser Strasse 4 • Map J1 • 01 409 1815 • Dis. access • No credit cards • €*

3 Café Weimar
Traditional café-restaurant with hot and cold snacks and a set lunch at midday. *Währinger Strasse 68 • Map B2 • 01 317 1206 • €€*

4 D'Landsknecht
A long-established local favourite: expect hearty portions of authentic Austrian soups and main dishes at moderate prices. *Porzellangasse 13 • Map B3 • 01 317 4348 • Closed Sat & Sun • €*

5 Gasthaus Wickerl
A very authentic Viennese restaurant with good Austrian cuisine. *Porzellangasse 24a • Map B3 • 01 317 7489 • Dis. access • No credit cards • €€€*

6 Stomach
A perennial Vienna favourite, Stomach serves modern food and has one of the nicest outdoor dining areas in the city. *Seegasse 26 • Map B3 • 01 310 2099 • €€€€*

7 Oasia
Dim sum is a speciality at this modern Asian-fusion restaurant with a sushi bar and open kitchen. *Schlickgasse 2 • Map B4 • 01 310 01 70 • Closed Sun • €€*

8 Servitenstüberl
A friendly family-run restaurant with Viennese specialities. It is located next to Servitenkirche *(see p99)* and has pleasant seating on the square overlooking the church in summer. *Servitengasse 7 • Map B4 • 01 317 5336 • €€*

9 Dreiklang
This vegetarian restaurant uses only organic products for its dishes and serves a midday menu. *Wasagasse 28 • Map C3 • 01 310 1703 • No credit cards • €€*

10 Ragusa
Dalmatian cooking (specialities include grilled fish and seafood) in a cosy atmosphere with outdoor seating. *Berggasse 15 • Map B3 • 01 317 1577 • Dis. access • €€€*

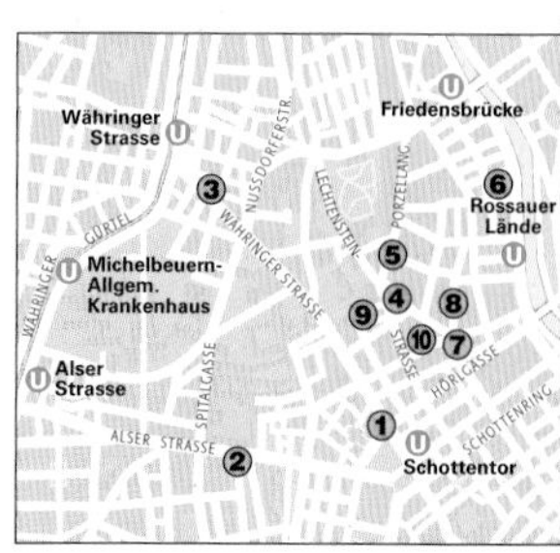

Note: *Unless otherwise stated, all restaurants accept credit cards and serve vegetarian meals*

Left **Museumsquartier** Right **Naturhistorisches Museum**

Town Hall and Museumsquartier

THE AREA AROUND THE TOWN HALL AND MUSEUMS QUARTER *is both the political centre of Austria and the cultural heart of the capital, with a number of world-class exhibition spaces. Bordered by Alser Strasse in the north and Mariahilfer Strasse in the south, the neighbourhood is also a popular residential area with beautiful houses in quiet streets and many shops and restaurants.*

Museumsquartier statue

TOP 10 Sights

1. Kunsthistorisches Museum
2. Museumsquartier
3. Naturhistorisches Museum
4. Neues Rathaus
5. Parliament
6. Spittelberg
7. Museum für Volkskunde
8. Volkstheater
9. Piaristenkirche Maria Treu
10. Sankt-Ulrichs-Platz

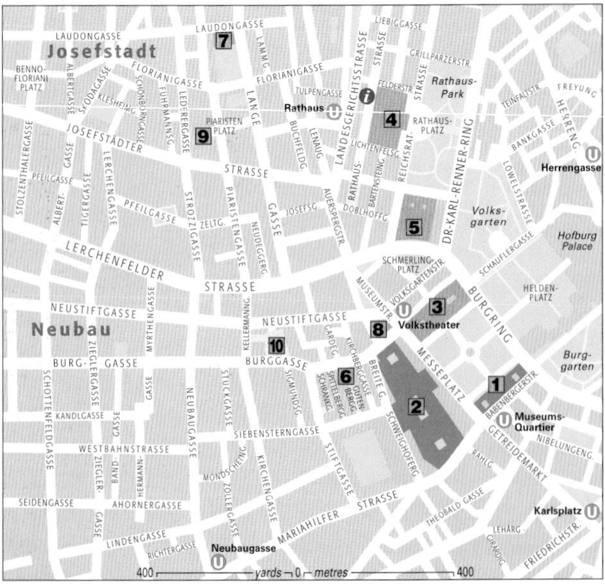

Kunsthistorisches Museum façade

1 Kunsthistorisches Museum

Vienna's Museum of Fine Art is home to an impressive collection of artistic treasures, spanning the centuries from the ancient world to the modern day *(see pp18–21)*.

2 Museumsquartier

The former imperial stables have been imaginatively transformed into a vast complex of museums and entertainment venues that shouldn't be missed *(see pp28–9)*.

3 Naturhistorisches Museum

Designed by Gottfried Semper and Karl von Hasenauer, who also worked on the Kunsthistorisches Museum, the Natural History Museum opened in 1889 and was built as a mirror image of its more famous neighbour, the Art History Museum. The fascinating collections of natural history, geology and archaeology have grown out of Emperor Franz Stephan's 1748 collection of natural curiosities. The museum's splendid interior was designed to enhance the objects, which today amount to more than 20 million exhibits. The most precious rarities in the museum's 39 showrooms are the 25,000-year-old Venus of Willendorf figurine and a "bouquet of jewels" given to Franz Stephan by his wife Maria Theresa. The Vienna Natural History Museum is often voted among the world's top 10 museums. *Burgring 7 • Map K4 • Open 9am–6:30pm Thu–Mon, 9am–9pm Wed • Dis. access • Adm (free for under 19s) • www.nhm-wien.ac.at*

4 Neues Rathaus

The Neo-Gothic town hall with its spires, stone rosettes in the pointed windows and loggias was built by Friedrich von Schmidt in 1883 to express the inhabitants' pride in their city at that time. The impressive building has seven arcaded courtyards and 1,575 rooms, where the Vienna City Council and the mayor have their offices. All year round various festivals take place on the square in front of the Rathaus, ranging from a Christmas market to a music film festival in summer *(see p80)*. Don't miss the opportunity to see the building at night, when floodlights spectacularly highlight the façade. *Rathausplatz • Map J2 • Guided tours (German only) 1pm Mon, Wed & Fri • Free • www.wien.gv.at*

Neues Rathaus

5 Parliament

This building (1873–83) was designed by the architect Theophil von Hansen in Greek style to celebrate the cradle of democracy. Two broad ramps are lined by statues of Greek philosophers leading to the main entrance. Here the first Austrian Republic was declared in 1918. *Dr-Karl-Renner-Ring 3 • Map K3 • Tours on the hour 11am & 2–4pm Mon–Thu; 11am & 1–4pm Fri; 11am–4pm Sat (mid-Jun–mid-Sep: 11am–4pm Mon–Sat) • Dis. access • Adm*

Spittelberg courtyard

6 Spittelberg

The charming Spittelberg area consists of a few cobbled, narrow streets with pretty houses and spouting fountains between Breite Gasse, Siebensterngasse, Sigmundsgasse and Burggasse. In the 18th century the area was full of hovels, gambling dens and brothels, but by the 19th century these establishments had been closed down and, over the course of time, the district became increasingly derelict. The city authorities only began to recognize the area's charm in the 1970s, and today it's a thriving enclave of galleries, handicraft shops and cosy pubs. *Map J5*

Ringstrasse

The Ringstrasse encircles the city's first district and, with its many representative buildings, is one of the world's most elegant avenues. In December 1857 Emperor Franz Joseph I gave orders to tear down the city's medieval strongholds and give Vienna an imperial face with bombastic edifices. Vienna's nobility then built palaces along the new boulevard that was officially opened in 1865.

7 Museum für Volkskunde

The fine Baroque Schönborn Palace, built between 1708 and 1713 by Lukas von Hildebrandt, has been the home of the Austrian Museum of Folk Life and Folk Art since 1917. Besides changing exhibitions, it features a permanent collection of traditional Austrian clothing, furniture, pottery, religious objects and tools dating from the 17th to the 19th centuries. The museum, founded in 1895, also includes collections from the former territory of the Austro-Hungarian Empire. The palace has wonderful landscaped gardens that can also be accessed without visiting the museum. *Laudongasse 15–19 • Map C2 • Open 10am–5pm Tue–Sun • Adm*

8 Volkstheater

The Volkstheater ("people's theatre") was established in 1889 as a counterpart to the imperial Burgtheater *(see p85)*. Its aim was to offer classic and modern drama to a larger audience at reasonable prices. Built by the acclaimed theatre architects Ferdinand Fellner and Hermann Helmer, the theatre was designed in Historicist style and fitted with what was then the latest technology and security measures, such as electric lighting. With just under 1,000 seats, the Volkstheater is among the largest German-language theatres in the world. *Neustiftgasse 1 • Map J4*

You must have a photo ID with you to enter the Parliament building

Volkstheater

9 Piaristenkirche Maria Treu

Walking into the narrow Piaristengasse from Josefstädter Strasse, the charming square on the left comes as a surprise. The Piaristenkirche Maria Treu (Maria Treu Church) here was built from 1719 onwards according to a design by Lukas von Hildebrandt. The dome's frescoes in vivid colours are by the Austrian Baroque artist Franz Anton Maulbertsch (1752), while the column in front of the church, the Mariensäule, was installed in 1713 to express gratitude that a plague epidemic had come to an end. *Jodok Fink Platz • Map D2 • Open during church services • Free*

10 Sankt-Ulrichs-Platz

At the heart of this charming cobbled square is St Ulrich's Church, which is surrounded by a pretty ensemble of patrician houses dating back to various periods. At No. 5 is a rare example of a Renaissance house, while the Baroque edifice at No. 27 bears a statue of St Nepomuk, who gave the house its name, tucked away in a little niche. During the Turkish Siege of 1683, Kara Mustafa's troops pitched their tents on this square. *Map E2*

Saint Nepomuk statue, Sankt Ulrichs-Platz

A Walk around the Museums Quarter

Morning

Begin your day at the **Neues Rathaus** *(see p103)*, then leisurely walk along the Ringstrasse towards **Parliament**. Once you have taken in these political gems, you are then free to explore the city's wonderful museums.

The highlights are the **Kunsthistorisches Museum** *(see pp18–21)* and **Naturhistorisches Museum** *(see p103)* and you could easily spend a full day in each of the museums, so select your main areas of interest and concentrate on those collections. Have a morning coffee in the museums themselves – the cafés in both venues are excellent and offer a great view of the museums' lower floors.

Walk across the square to the **Museumsquartier** *(see pp28–9)* and stroll around the many courtyards. Before embarking on another museum, have lunch in any of the four restaurants in the complex – all of them offer equally delicious food.

Afternoon

After lunch, visit the Museum for Modern Art and the Leopold Museum, before leaving the complex through gates 6 or 7. These lead you straight to the **Volkstheater**. Make your way up Burggasse and the **Spittelberg** area spills out to your left, where you can stroll around the shops and galleries.

After dark, return to the Neues Rathaus to see it lit up against the night sky.

Left **Grand Cru** Right **Austrian wine label**

TOP 10 Specialist Shops

1 Quendler's feine Weine

The top address in Vienna for fine red and white Austrian wines, including Riesling, as well as wines from around the world. *Schmidgasse 8 • Map D2*

Riesling wine label

6 PerydShou

This specialist shop can print images onto almost anything, from the more usual T-shirts, caps and bags to lamps, glass, plates and cups. *Zollergasse 9 • Map E2*

2 Grand Cru

This shop offers a great selection of coffees, both Viennese and international, as well as delicious chocolates with a variety of tasty fillings. *Kaiserstrasse 67*

3 Artee

A wide range of teas, complemented by stylish teapots and cups from all over the world, all set in an equally elegant atmosphere. Authentic Asian food with dim sum variations served all day. *Siebensterngasse 4 • Map E2*

4 Bag and Art

Specialists in leather handbags and leather gloves, Bag and Art also hosts changing exhibitions in the shop. *Neubaugasse 49 • Map E2*

5 Mastnak

This beautiful stationery shop has everything from plain cards to celebrate any occasion to beautiful wrapping paper, decorated diaries and fountain pens. The ideal place for gifts. *Neubaugasse 31 • Map E2*

7 Vinoe

Top wines from the wine-growing region of Lower Austria are on sale here at reasonable prices. *Piaristengasse 35 • Map D2*

8 Das Möbel

A mixture between a furniture gallery, café and restaurant where you can test out the comfort of the furniture while having a drink or a meal. The design of the interior changes every three months. *Burggasse 10 • Map E2*

9 Shu!

Shoes in unusual colours, shoes with extraordinary heels, shoes with bizarre buckles – a veritable footwear paradise. All the styles are created by international and Austrian designers. *Neubaugasse 34 • Map E2*

10 Sax & Co

Behind the very pretty shopfront is another beautiful stationery shop selling handmade paper and writing equipment. *Neubaugasse 34 • Map E2*

Above **Tunnel**

Price Categories

For a three-course meal for one with half a bottle of wine (or equivalent meal), taxes and extra charges.

€	under €25
€€	€25–€35
€€€	€35–€55
€€€€	€55–€70
€€€€€	over €70

TOP 10 Places to Eat

1 Amerling Beisl
Vines hang from the dark wooden balcony in the idyllic Biedermeier-style courtyard garden here, while the inside is modern. *Stiftgasse 8 • Map E2 • 01 526 1660 • Dis access • €€*

2 Die Wäscherei
This former laundry is one of the hotspots in the area. It has delicious brunch at weekends but book ahead. *Albertgasse 49 • Map C1 • 01 409 23 7511 • Dis access • €€*

3 Plutzer Bräu
A pub with traditional Viennese food. In summer there is seating outside. *Schrankgasse 2 • Map E2 • 01 526 1215 • €€*

4 Café Lux
Lux, in the Spittelberg area, offers creative cuisine and has seating in the inner courtyard. *Schrankgasse 4, Spittelberggasse 3 • Map E2 • 01 526 9491 • €€€*

5 Tunnel
International food with many Oriental dishes is on the menu here. There is live music daily in the cellar. *Florianigasse 39 • Map D1 • 01 405 3465 • No credit cards • €*

6 Zu ebener Erde und erster Stock
Located on the ground and first floors of a beautiful Biedermeier-style house, this eatery serves creative and traditional Austrian cuisine and fine wines. *Burggasse 13 • Map E2 • 01 523 6254 • €€€*

7 Witwe Bolte
This cosy spot in the Spittelberg area has outdoor seating in summer and offers refined Viennese cuisine and Austrian wines. *Gutenberggasse 13 • Map J5 • 01 523 1450 • Dis. access • €€€*

8 Prinz Ferdinand
A typical Viennese restaurant with classic Austrian specialities. In summer there is romantic seating underneath trees on the square. *Bennoplatz 2 • Map D1 • 01 402 9417 • Closed Mon • Dis. access • €€€*

9 Beim Novak
Serving sophisticated Viennese cuisine, Beim Novak has lovely seating on the veranda of this 200-year-old house. *Richtergasse 12 • Map F1 • 01 523 3244 • Closed Sat–Sun, Aug • €€€*

10 Gaumenspiel
Inventive dishes such as lobster ravioli are served on a regularly changing menu. *Zieglergasse 54 • Map E1 • 01 526 1108 • €€€*

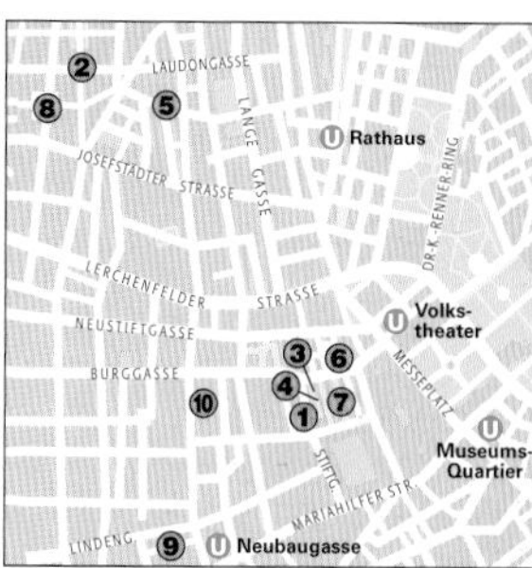

Note: *Unless otherwise stated, all restaurants accept credit cards and serve vegetarian meals*

Left **Naschmarkt** Right **Secession building**

Opera and Naschmarkt

THIS IS A MULTIFACETED AREA, featuring many architectural landmarks standing regally alongside the colourful activity of the Naschmarkt. It is characterized by great buildings of various styles such as the historic State Opera House and the Academy of Fine Arts, as well as the finest examples of Viennese Art Nouveau with the Secession Building and two stunning Otto Wagner houses on Linke Wienzeile. The area is also a shoppers' paradise – Mariahilfer Strasse boasts hundreds of stores and many cafés and restaurants, while the Naschmarkt offers a different kind of retail experience. The lively market with eclectic stalls bears some resemblance to Oriental bazaars and is a delight for all the senses.

Balcony, Theater an der Wien

Top 10 Sights

1. Staatsoper
2. Secession Building
3. Akademie der bildenden Künste
4. Naschmarkt
5. Majolika Haus
6. Wagner Haus
7. Schiller Monument
8. Mariahilfer Strasse
9. Theater an der Wien
10. The Imperial Furniture Collection

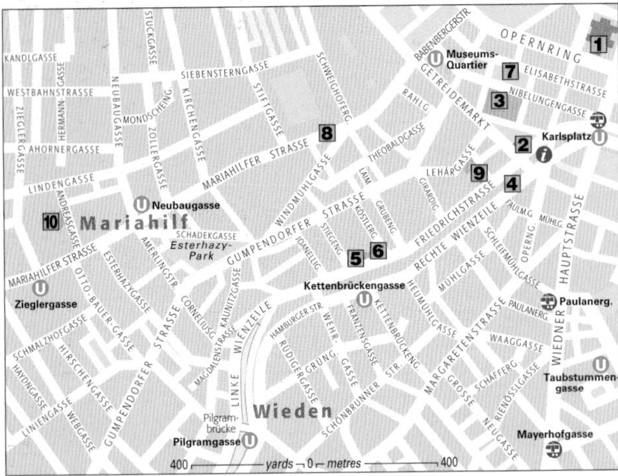

Staatsoper façade

1 Staatsoper

The Vienna State Opera House is a landmark in a city that loves its music, and has witnessed the premieres of many world-famous works *(see pp30–31)*.

2 Secession Building

This remarkable late 19th-century building is a celebration of the Secessionist artistic movement *(see pp32–3)*.

3 Akademie der bildenden Künste

When the medieval bastions around the inner city were knocked down at the end of the 19th century and the Ringstrasse was laid out, Theophil von Hansen constructed a building in the Italian Renaissance style in 1872–6 to house Vienna's art school. The school, founded by Peter Strudel in 1692, moved here from the Strudelhof building on the academy's completion. The Academy of Fine Arts became internationally famous for its training of painters, sculptors, architects, graphic artists and stage designers. It also houses a gallery of 17th-century Dutch and Flemish Old Masters, 19th-century Austrian works, and a huge collection of copper etchings *(see p44)*. *Schillerplatz 3 • Map L6 • Open 10am–6pm Tue–Sun • Adm • www.akademiegalerie.at*

4 Naschmarkt

Naschmarkt, the city's largest market, is a colourful place with hundreds of stalls. Life here starts at 6am, when vendors selling fruit, vegetables, flowers, meat and fish open their stalls. At weekends farmers from outside the city offer their produce, and at the Saturday flea market makeshift stalls sell everything from antiques to second-hand clothing. *Between Karlsplatz and Kettenbrückengasse • Map F4 • Open 6am–7:30pm Mon–Fri, 6am–5pm Sat*

5 Majolika Haus

One of the finest examples of an Art Nouveau-style house was designed by the celebrated architect Otto Wagner in 1898. The house is decorated with colourful floral patterns on glazed tiles – pink roses, green leaves and blue blossoms spread across the building's weather-resistant surface. The windowsills bear matching floral patterns. The house is now divided into apartments with shops on the ground floor. *Linke Wienzeile 40 • Map F3*

Majolika Haus

Arrive early on Saturday morning if you want to rummage through the Naschmarkt flea market without large crowds

A Musical City

Vienna is tightly connected to classical music and is often referred to as the world's musical capital. The art-loving Habsburgs functioned as paymasters and provided the perfect setting for a flourishing musical landscape, particularly from the late 18th to the 19th centuries. Today the tradition of its rich past remains, but there is also a vivid scene of contemporary music in the city.

6 Wagner Haus

Next to the Majolika House is another of Otto Wagner's Art Nouveau-style buildings. The six-storey house has a white plastered façade with beautiful golden stucco elements. Between the top row of windows are golden medallions with female heads, designed by Wagner's fellow artist Koloman Moser (1868–1918). Golden palm leaves are spread above the medallions and peacock feathers underneath reach down to the windows below. Above the rounded corner with an iron-and-glass porch are statues of female "callers" by Othmar Schimkowitz (1864–1947). Some of the designs are from Wagner's students who also became well-known architects, such as Josef Maria Olbrich, the Secession Building's architect. *Linke Wienzeile 38 • Map F3*

Schiller Monument

7 Schiller Monument

The focal point of Schillerplatz, the square in front of the Academy of Fine Arts, is the statue of the poet and dramatist Friedrich Schiller, sculpted by Johannes Schilling in 1876. Opposite is the Goethe monument, created by Edmund Hellmer in 1900 *(see p54)* as a tribute to the two great German-language writers. *Schillerplatz • Map L6*

8 Mariahilfer Strasse

After Kärntner Strasse and the Graben, this pedestrianized street is the city's trendiest and busiest shopping mile. Hundreds of shops and a few department stores offer fashion, books, music and electronic goods, while cafés, restaurants, ice cream parlours and cinemas abound. The shops are interspersed with two churches, Stiftskirche at the lower end and Mariahilf in the middle. *Map K6*

Wagner Haus façade

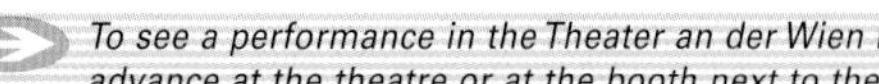

To see a performance in the Theater an der Wien buy tickets in advance at the theatre or at the booth next to the Staatsoper

9 Theater an der Wien

Emanuel Schikaneder, a friend of Mozart, had this theatre built between 1798 and 1801, but only one year after its grand opening he went bankrupt and sold the building. The theatre has had a colourful history, changing owners many times, but saw great historic moments with the premiere of Beethoven's *Fidelio* in 1805 and Johann Strauss's operetta *Die Fledermaus* in 1874. The theatre closed down in 1938, but after World War II it staged state opera performances while the damaged Staatsoper was being repaired. Today, having staged musicals for so long, it is now once again an opera house. *Linke Wienzeile 6 • Map F3*

10 The Imperial Furniture Collection

In the *Hofmobiliendepot* (imperial court furniture repository), which was established by Empress Maria Theresa in the late 18th century, all the Habsburgs' furniture was stored, repaired and kept in a good state to be distributed to imperial households whenever required. Today the museum tells how imperial families used to live and has thousands of exhibits spanning more than five centuries. Among them are curiosities such as Baroque armchairs on wheels, an imperial travel throne, velvet-covered praying stools, Rococo spittoons and toilets disguised as stacks of books. There are also fully furnished rooms on display ranging from Empress Elisabeth's rustic rooms from the Schönbrunn Meierei and a typical girl's room as it would have looked in the Biedermeier period. *Andreasgasse 7 • Map F1 • Open 10am–6pm Tue–Sun • Adm • www.hofmobiliendepot.at*

A Day in the Opera and Naschmarkt Area

Morning

Starting off by admiring the impressive **Staatsoper** *(see pp30–31)*, cut your way through Operngasse to the **Secession Building** *(see pp32–3)*. The stunning *Beethoven Frieze* inside this Art Nouveau building shouldn't be missed. The **Akademie der bildenden Künste** *(see p109)* is just a stone's throw from Olbrich's Secessionist masterpiece and is also worth an hour or two, particularly for its fine Rubens paintings.

For a coffee, head for the refurbished **Café Museum** *(see p114)*, first designed by Adolf Loos in 1899.

Walk towards **Naschmarkt** *(see p109)* and roam the market with all its stalls and lively atmosphere, casting a glance over the road to the **Theater an der Wien**, the **Majolika Haus** *(see p109)* and the **Wagner Haus**.

For lunch, choose from one of the cafés or restaurants on Naschmarkt such as the **Do An** *(see p115)*.

Afternoon

Make your way up to **Mariahilfer Strasse** and spend the rest of the afternoon leisurely looking around the many shops.

Stay in the area for the evening and attend a classical opera performance either in the Staatsoper or in the Theater an der Wien. But, whichever of the two entertainment venues you choose, make sure you have booked your tickets in advance.

Following pages **Majolika Haus**

Left **Café Museum** Right **Wein & Co Bar**

Top 10 Cafés and Bars

1 Café Drechsler
Elegantly remodelled by UK architects Conran & Partners, this legendary coffee house has regained its mantel as the place in Vienna for a late, late night drink or an early, early breakfast! *Linke Wienzeile 22 • Map F2*

2 Wein & Co Bar
Just opposite the Secession Building *(see pp32–3)*, this trendy place is not only a wine shop but also a bar with more than 60 wines from all across the globe. It also serves Italian cuisine. *Getreidemarkt 1 • Map L6*

3 Café Sperl
This café has been in business for more than 120 years and has a reputation for being frequented by the city's artists, actors and nobles. It is just as popular today as it has always been *(see p77)*. *Gumpendorfer Strasse 11 • Map K6*

4 Barfly's Club
Situated in the Hotel Fürst Metternich, this stylish bar has a huge selection of cocktails, whiskies and rums, as well as live jazz and swing music. *Esterhazygasse 33 • Map F2*

5 Café Ritter
A traditional café just off the main shopping drag with the obligatory variety of coffees, cakes, snacks and newspapers. A great break from nearby shopping. *Mariahilfer Strasse 73 • Map F2*

6 Naschmarkt Deli
This little café amid the bustling Naschmarkt market stalls serves excellent breakfasts all day long and offers all kinds of ethnic cuisines, from Viennese to Turkish. *Naschmarkt stall 421–36 • Map F4*

7 Tanzcafé Jenseits
It would be easy to walk right past this very cosy bar. Its plush reddish decor has a slightly faded, Hollywood-of-yesteryear feel, and there is a small dance floor. *Nelkengasse 3 • Map F2*

8 Café Museum
Adolf Loos's minimalist-designed coffee house makes a great place to people-watch and soak up the atmosphere while enjoying coffee and cake *(see p77)*. *Operngasse 7 • Map M5*

9 Cafe Franz
This cosy coffee house located close to the Naschmarkt offers late breakfasts, pancakes with a variety of toppings and fillings, and excellent beers. *Pressgasse 29 • Map F3*

10 Roxy
If staying up all night is your thing, head to Roxy, which opens when most other places in the city close. With live DJ music in a relaxed bar atmosphere, there is also a dance floor. *Operngasse 24 on the corner of Faulmanngasse • Map F4*

Price Categories

For a three-course meal for one with half a bottle of wine (or equivalent meal), taxes and extra charges.

€	under €25
€€	€25–€35
€€€	€35–€55
€€€€	€55–€70
€€€€€	over €70

Above **Theatercafé**

Top 10 Places to Eat

1 Umarfisch

Sample the delicious oysters and a glass of sparkling wine. *Naschmarkt Stand 76–9 • Map F3 • 01 587 04 56 • Dis. access • €€€*

2 Do An

Do An prepares a varied cuisine – the smoked tofu with sautéed courgettes, carrots and spring onions is delicious. *Naschmarkt stall 412 • Map F4 • 01 585 82 53 • No credit cards • €€*

3 Theatercafé

Austrian cuisine with Asian and Italian influences. Usually crowded after performances at the Theater an der Wien next door. *Linke Wienzeile 6 • Map F3 • 01 585 62 62 • Dis. access • €€€*

4 Salzberg

In a traditional setting, Salzberg serves creative Viennese dishes and beer brewed in eastern Austria for the restaurant. *Magdalenenstrasse 17 • Map G2 • 01 581 62 26 • Dis. access • €€€*

5 Zu den drei Buchteln

This cosy place serves Bohemian specialities such as yeast cakes known as *Buchteln*. *Wehrgasse 9 • Map G3 • 01 587 83 65 • Closed Sun • No credit cards • €€€*

6 Steman

Diners eat at long tables at this cosy restaurant serving traditional Viennese fare. *Otto-Bauer Gasse 7 • Map F1 • 01 597 85 09 • Dis. access • Closed Sat & Sun • €€€*

7 Indian Pavilion

The smallest Indian restaurant in Vienna, but certainly the best. Try the lentil soup, then the divine mango pickle with a curry. Get there early as it fills up quickly. *Naschmarkt 74–5 • Map F3 • 01 587 85 61 • Dis. access • Closed evenings • €€*

8 Café Amarcord

A very relaxed place with leather sofas – perfect after the hectic Naschmarkt. Tasty food from Viennese to vegetarian. *Rechte Wienzeile 15 • Map F3 • 01 587 47 09 • No credit cards • €€€*

9 Restaurant Sopile

A Croatian restaurant with a strong emphasis on fish dishes as well as truffles and game. Excellent wine list. *Paulanergasse 10 • Map F4 • 01 585 24 33 • Closed Sun and pub hols • €€€€*

10 Chang Asian Noodles

This noodle bar has a fresh and modern feel, and is always busy. It serves simple Asian food at reasonable prices. The weekly lunchtime set menus are a bargain. *Waaggasse 1 • Map F4 • 01 961 92 12 • Dis. access • €*

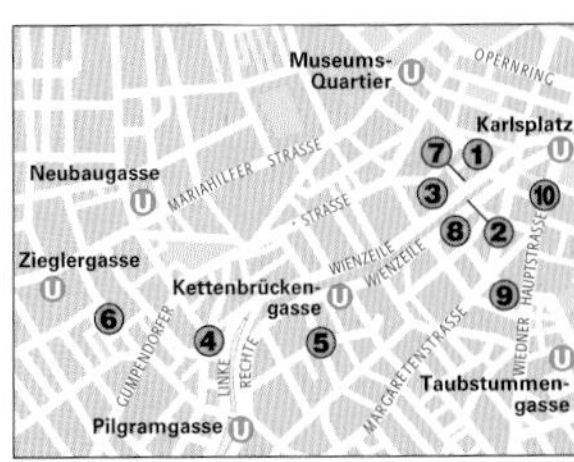

Note: *Unless otherwise stated, all restaurants accept credit cards and serve vegetarian meals*

Left **Musikvereinsgebäude** Right **Lower Belvedere**

From Karlskirche to the Belvedere

THE AREA FROM THE KARLSKIRCHE to the Belvedere Palace is predominantly filled with grand mansions and summer residences from the 18th and 19th centuries. Vienna's aristocracy built their summer palaces in this area because it was in the countryside but not too distant from the city. Prince Eugen's summer retreat, the Belvedere, clearly dominates the area, but there are several other ornate homes, such as the Palais Schwarzenberg and the Palais Hoyos, which are well worth a visit. Today many of these buildings function as embassies and some of the once private large gardens are now public parks. But the area is also known for its private schools, such as the Theresianum, and its many churches of various denominations. During Roman times the civil settlement of the military camp Vindobona (see p40) *was situated here and the main roads in the area, Landstrasser Hauptstrasse and Rennweg, follow old Roman routes.*

Salesiannerinnenkirche

Top 10 Sights

1. Karlskirche
2. The Belvedere
3. Musikverein
4. Otto Wagner Pavilion
5. Gardekirche
6. Salesianerinnenkirche
7. Schwarzenberggarten
8. Theresianum
9. Palais Hoyos
10. Liberation Monument

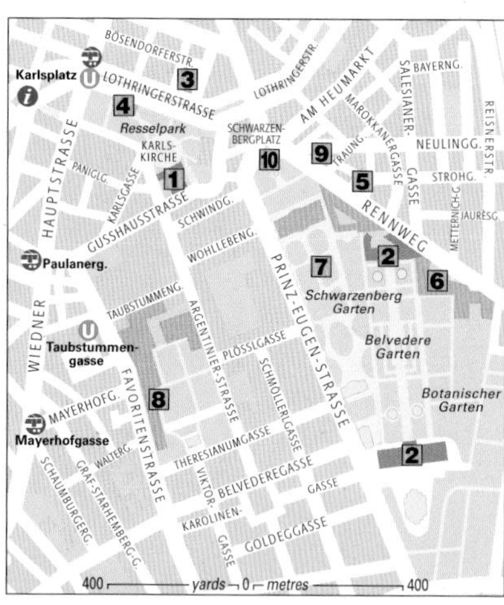

Karlskirche

1 Karlskirche

This Baroque masterpiece is one of Vienna's most impressive churches, with its beautiful carved columns and vast green dome *(see pp26–7)*.

2 The Belvedere

These two 18th-century palace buildings are beautifully linked by landscaped gardens filled with statuary *(see pp22–5)*.

3 Musikverein

This magnificent concert hall in Greek Renaissance style was built by Theophil von Hansen in 1869 for the Society of Friends of Music. The concert hall became world-famous after the Vienna Philharmonic Orchestra began giving their annual New Year's Concert here in 1941. There are three performance areas, but the main auditorium, the "Golden Hall", is the finest, with lavish decorations in blue and gold and excellent acoustics *(see p60)*.

Bösendorferstrasse 12 • Map N6 • Call 01 505 81 90 in advance for guided tours • Dis. access • Adm • www.musikverein.at

4 Otto Wagner Pavilion

The two pavilions on Karlsplatz were built by Otto Wagner in 1897 as twin stations for the Vienna City Train, the horse-drawn and then steam-powered predecessors of today's underground. In total Wagner designed 34 stations and various bridges and viaducts for the train line that was finished in 1901. The pavilions on Karlsplatz are made of steel and marble slabs, and the roof over the arched gate is decorated with golden ornaments. Both stations lost their function as the modern underground lines were built. Today they are used as exhibition spaces by the Wien Museum and as a café. *Karlsplatz • Map F4 • Exhibition: Open Apr–Oct: 10am–6pm Tue–Sun & public holidays • Adm*

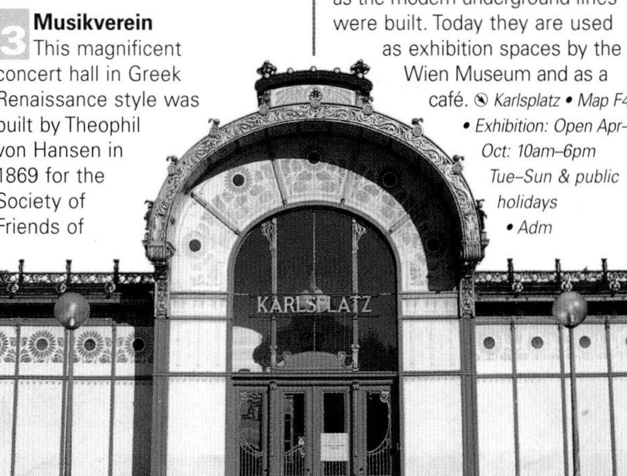

Otto Wagner Pavilion

Otto Wagner

Before Otto Wagner (1841–1918) became one of the most distinguished Viennese architects and an advocate of functional architecture, he was a Classical Revivalist. He moved from the Neo-Renaissance style to modernity by rejecting traditional brick for steel structures. No other architect has left such a strong imprint on the city.

5 Gardekirche

The construction of this Rococo church was decreed by Empress Maria Theresa in 1755, and her favourite architect Nikolaus von Pacassi (1716–90) completed the building in 1763. The plain, cubic structure with a red tiled roof and a green cupola was the church to the nearby military hospital. The interior is decorated with elaborate stucco work, and behind the high altar is the painting *Christ on the Crucifix* by Peter Strudel, the founder of Vienna's first art school. The church has been the Polish national church in Vienna since 1897. *Rennweg 5a • Map F5*

6 Salesianerinnenkirche

Amalia Wilhelmina (1673–1742), the wife of Emperor Josef I, founded this monastery of the Salesian convent in 1717 in thanks for her recovery from smallpox. The architect Donato Felice d'Allio completed the complex with its eight courtyards in 1728 and, together with the Belvedere and Palais Schwarzenberg, it forms a fine Baroque ensemble. The dome is decorated with frescoes by the Rococo painter Antonio Pellegrini (1675–1741) showing Mary's ascension to heaven. According to Amalia Wilhelmina's will, her body is buried under the high altar, but an urn with her heart was placed inside her husband's coffin in the imperial crypt on Neuer Markt. *Rennweg 8–10 • Map F6 • Closed to the public except during services 7am Mon–Sat, 9am Sun*

7 Schwarzenberggarten

In 1697, the Baroque architect Lukas von Hildebrandt was commissioned to build a summer palace here, which was bought by the influential Schwarzenberg family in 1720. Architects Johann Bernhard Fischer von Erlach and his son Joseph Emanuel continued adorning the palace and laid out the garden in formal French style. *Schwarzenbergplatz 9 • Map F5 • Closed to the public*

8 Theresianum

On the site of this elite school stood an imperial summer palace, until it was destroyed by Turkish troops in 1683. On its ruins the Italian architect Lodovico Burnacini built the Theresianum (1687–90). The long building with a sober façade was named after

Theresianum façade

Although the Gardekirche is closed unless there are services, you can step into the entrance area and get a look inside the church

Liberation Monument

Empress Maria Theresa, who installed an educational institute here for young nobility. Today it is a private school and a diplomatic academy. *Favoritenstrasse 15 • Map G4 • Closed to the public*

9 Palais Hoyos

Otto Wagner built this Neo-Renaissance palace as his home in 1891, before he joined the Secessionist movement. The windows of the upper floor are framed with floral details, but the ground and first floors are built in sombre stone. *Rennweg 3 • Map F5 • Closed to the public*

10 Liberation Monument

The Liberation Monument of the Red Army is a reminder of Vienna's postwar history, when the city was occupied by the four Allied Powers and divided into four zones. Schwarzenbergplatz was part of the Soviet zone and renamed Stalinplatz. The monument was installed in 1945; at the end of Allied occupation in 1955, the republic pledged to maintain the monument. *Schwarzenbergplatz • Map F5*

A Day's Walk from Karlsplatz to the Belvedere

Morning

Start your day at Karlsplatz, where you can inspect the Otto Wagner pavilions in Resselpark and then walk on to the **Karlskirche** *(see pp26–7)*. Left of the church is the **Wien Museum Karlsplatz** *(see p43)*, where you could easily spend a few hours studying the city's history. Don't miss the Klimt and Schiele paintings, as well as Adolf Loos's original living room from 1903.

Head towards Argentinierstrasse, right of Karlskirche, where you can enjoy a coffee in **Café Goldegg** *(see p120)*.

Walk east to the **Liberation Monument**, then take Rennweg and pass by Otto Wagner's **Palais Hoyos**. For lunch, pop into **Salm Bräu** *(see p120)*.

Afternoon

It is now time to head for the **Belvedere** *(see pp22–5)*, where you could spend the rest of the day. After having a look at the exhibition in the Lower Belvedere, walk through the formal gardens towards the Upper Belvedere, home to the Austrian National Gallery with many Schiele, Klimt, Gerstl and Attersee paintings. You can also visit the 21er Haus gallery on Arsenalstrasse 1, about 10 minutes' walk from here. It holds changing exhibitions of Austrian art from 1945 to the present day.

Consider attending a concert in the **Konzerthaus** *(see p60)*, but you need to book a day in advance.

Left **Café Schwarzenberg** Right **Salm Bräu**

Top 10 Cafés and Bars

1 Café Schwarzenberg
A traditional Viennese café with opulent red velvet seating and mirrors on the walls. In summer, seating is on a terrace facing the Ringstrasse. The café hosts changing exhibitions of Viennese artists and there are piano concerts on Wednesday and Friday evenings (7:30–10pm). *Kärntner Ring 17 • Map N6 • Dis. access*

2 High Tea
This teahouse, bar and restaurant rolled into one has a stylish atmosphere. Besides teas from around the world, High Tea serves breakfast and light set lunches. There are also two Internet workstations, and in the adjoining shop you can choose from about 200 varieties of tea. *Paniglgasse 17 • Map F4 • Closed Sun • Dis. access*

3 Café Goldegg
A peaceful café and a retreat for reading the daily papers. There is a games room where you can play chess or cards. *Argentinierstrasse 49/corner of Goldeggasse • Map H5*

4 Silver Bar at the Hotel Triest
With its cool, laid-back vibe and first-class cocktails, the Silver Bar has long been the choice of Vienna's hip crowd. Enjoy a relaxed drink in its opulent surroundings. *Wiedner Haupstrasse 12 • Map F4 • Dis. access*

5 Café Wortner
Great historic coffee house with a whiff of the Biedermeier era about it; especially good for sitting outside. *Wiedner Hauptstrasse 55 • Map G4 • Dis. access*

6 Café Karl-Otto
Popular café/restaurant serving traditional food by day, and a club with international DJs by night. *Otto Wagner Pavilion, Karlsplatz • Map F4*

7 Flanagan's Irish Pub
Enjoy pints of Guinness here. The furniture was imported from a pub in Cork. *Schwarzenbergstrasse 1–3 • Map N5*

8 Salm Bräu
You not only get hearty dishes at Salm Bräu but they also brew their own beers. The food complements the ale – different sausage specialities and bread with various spreads. *Rennweg 8 • Map F5 • Dis. access*

9 Point of Sale
This designer café serves all kinds of international breakfasts until late into the afternoon. *Schleifmühlgasse 12 • Map F4*

10 Artner Restaurant-Weinkellerei
A cosy wine bar and restaurant. Try home-made goat's cheese marinated in olive oil and herbs. You can take a bottle home with you from the wine boutique. *Floragasse 6 • Map G4 • Dis. access*

Above **Pan e Wien**

Price Categories

For a three-course meal for one with half a bottle of wine (or equivalent meal), taxes and extra charges.

€	under €25
€€	€25–€35
€€€	€35–€55
€€€€	€55–€70
€€€€€	over €70

Top 10 Places to Eat

1 Weinzirl

Enjoy dinner in the magnificent surroundings of the Art Nouveau Konzerthaus. Combine the delicacies on offer to form your own menu. *Am Heumarkt 6 • Map P6 • 01 512 55 50 • Dis. access • €€€€*

2 Pan e Wien

With emphasis on food and wine from Piedmont, this is one of Vienna's best Italian restaurants. *Salesianergasse 55 • Map F6 • 01 710 38 70 • Closed Sun eve • Dis. access • €€€€*

3 Gmoa Keller

Favoured by the musical fraternity from the nearby concert halls, Gmoa Keller serves seasonal dishes and good wines. *Am Heumarkt 25 • Map P6 • 01 712 53 10 • Closed Sun & pub hols • Dis. access • €€*

4 Fasanlwirt

Traditional Viennese dishes including *Gulasch* and *Schweinsbraten (see pp70–71)* feature here. *Rennweg 24 • Map F5 • 01 798 45 51 • Closed Sat • Dis. access • €€*

5 Bierreither

This restaurant specializes in spare ribs, which are prepared in no fewer than eight different ways. *Schwarzenbergplatz 3 • Map F5 • 01 715 71 69 • Dis. access • €€€*

6 Collio

Fine Italian cooking in a cool ambience (decor is by Terence Conran). Tables outside in summer. *Hotel Das Triest, Wiedner Hauptstrasse 12 • Map G4 • 01 589 18 133 • €€€€*

7 Gasthaus Ubl

Probably Vienna's last simply styled Gasthaus. Large portions of classic Viennese food are served in beautiful oak-panelled surroundings. Very popular with the locals. *Pressgasse 26 • Map F3 • 01 587 64 37 • No credit cards • €*

8 Zur Steirischen Botschaft

Dishes from Austria's southern province of Styria are served in this restaurant with a lovely garden. *Strohgasse 11 • Map F6 • 01 712 33 67 • Closed Sat, Sun eve; open for Sun lunch only in summer • Dis. access • €€*

9 Wieden Bräu

A restaurant serving Viennese food such as *Schnitzel* in beer dough and a brewery that produces its own beer on the premises. *Waaggasse 5 • Map G4 • 01 586 03 00 • Dis. access • €€*

10 Restaurant Sperl

The extensive menu at Sperl features Viennese and Austrian specialities. *Karolinengasse 13 • Map G5 • 01 504 73 34 • Dis. access • €€*

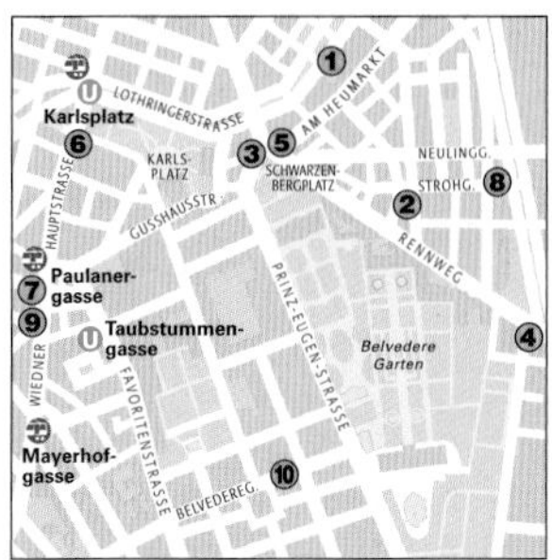

Note: *Unless otherwise stated, all restaurants accept credit cards and serve vegetarian meals*

Left **Hundertwasserhaus** Right **Dr-Karl-Lueger-Gedächtniskirche, Zentralfriedhof**

Greater Vienna

Detail, Hermesvilla

THE CITY OF VIENNA IS LOCATED *where the rolling hills of the Vienna Woods slope down into the Vienna basin, the Wiener Becken; from here it spreads out on both sides of the Danube. The Vienna Woods, to the west of the city, provide a welcome green belt and a peaceful backdrop and recreation area for city dwellers – it is a popular destination among the Viennese for short excursions and hikes. Today's suburbs such as Grinzing and Nussdorf were once separate countryside villages, until the spreading city swallowed them up as part of the Greater Vienna area. In the 17th and 18th centuries the city's rich and noble families built their summer residences and villas within easy reach of the capital, but far enough out to benefit from cool rural surroundings during the hottest time of the year. Schloss Schönbrunn, Geymüllerschlössel and Hermesvilla were grand summer houses of this type. Also away from the centre, for reasons of hygiene and space, is the country's largest cemetery, the Zentralfriedhof.*

Statue, Schönbrunn Park

Top 10 Sights

1. **Hundertwasserhaus**
2. **Schloss Schönbrunn**
3. **Hermesvilla**
4. **Kirche am Steinhof**
5. **Zentralfriedhof**
6. **Grinzing**
7. **Kahlenberg**
8. **Leopoldsberg**
9. **Geymüllerschlössel**
10. **Heiligenstädter Beethoven House**

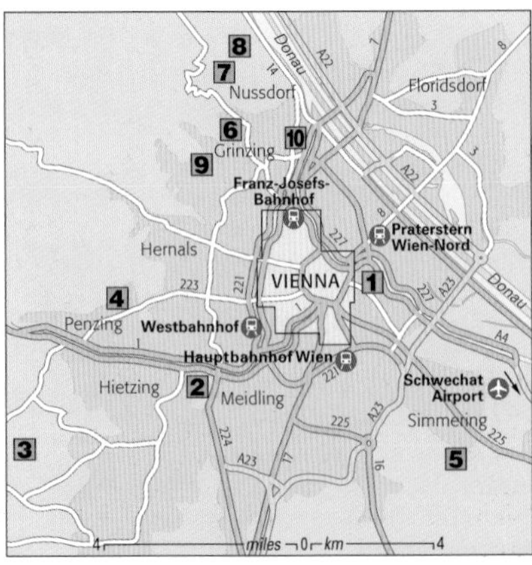

1 Hundertwasserhaus

Containing perhaps the most unusual and colourful private residences in the world, this apartment block was built in 1985 by the eccentric artist Friedensreich Hundertwasser *(see pp34–5)*.

2 Schloss Schönbrunn

This imperial Baroque palace with its stunning landscaped gardens is one of Vienna's most spectacular and most visited sights *(see pp36–9)*.

3 Hermesvilla

Situated on the former imperial hunting grounds of the Lainzer Tiergarten, Emperor Franz Joseph had this little palace built for his wife Elisabeth. Between 1882 and 1886 architect Karl von Hasenauer constructed the splendid villa with its opulent interior, and the imperial couple used to spend May and June here every year. Elisabeth's bedroom, with a large 18th-century bed once owned by Maria Theresa, is painted with frescoes following Hans Makart's designs of Shakespeare's comedy *A Midsummer Night's Dream.* The villa's name derives from the Hermes statue in the park. *Lainzer Tiergarten • Bus 60B to Lainzer Tor and a 15-min walk; U-Bahn U4 and a 2-hr walk • Open Apr–Oct: 10am–6pm Tue–Sun & public hols • Adm • www.wienmuseum.at*

4 Kirche am Steinhof

This church, another Art Nouveau masterpiece by Otto Wagner *(see p118)*, was created between 1905 and 1907 as a place of worship for the patients at the Steinhof psychiatric hospital. The entire hospital complex at the edge of the Vienna Woods was designed to bring the patients closer to a healthy and natural environment to help their recovery. The square church, flanked by two bell towers, was also intended to bring aesthetic pleasure to the sick. Its glistening golden dome can be spotted from the Gloriette building in Schönbrunn Park *(see p49)*. *Baumgartner Höhe 1 • Bus 47A, 48A • 01 910 60 11 007 • Open 4–5pm Sat, noon–4pm Sun • Guided tours: 3pm Sat, 4pm Sun & by appt • Adm (interior only)*

Schloss Schönbrunn

Grinzing

5 Zentralfriedhof

More than three million people have been buried in this 2.5-hectare (6-acre) cemetery since it opened in 1874, among them 500 Austrian politicians (there is a presidential crypt), composers and actors who were given honorary graves. Max Hegele, a student of Otto Wagner, designed the entrance portal (gate 2), the mortuary and the Dr-Karl-Lueger-Gedächtniskirche, named after a Vienna mayor (1897–1910). The church is among Vienna's most important Art Nouveau buildings. Within the cemetery there are separate areas for followers of the Jewish, Islamic, Orthodox and Protestant faiths. *Simmeringer Hauptstrasse 234, Tor 2 • Tram 71 • Open Mar–Apr & Sep–Oct: 7am–6pm; May–Aug: 7am–8pm; Nov–Feb: 8am–5pm • Free*

Vienna Woods

The Vienna Woods, which spread towards the west of the city, were turned into a protected area as early as 1467 by Emperor Friedrich III. Then the forest was not endangered by the roads being cut through the green belt but by people collecting firewood. During 19th-century industrialization, the forest was threatened with being cut down in a bid to gain resources, but today the Vienna Woods are as popular for excursions as ever.

6 Grinzing

Vienna is the only capital in the world where wine grapes are grown within the city boundaries – some 675 hectares (1,670 acres) of vineyards are found here. The most widely known wine-growing community in the capital is Grinzing. Once a small vintners' village on the outskirts of the city, it is today the hub of *Heurigen*, with crowds of both locals and tourists flocking to the wine taverns *(see pp74–5)*. The narrow streets still boast an old-fashioned rural charm. *U-Bahn U4, U6; Tram 38*

7 Kahlenberg

The 484-m- (1,580-ft-) high Kahlenberg mountain is on the fringe of the Vienna Woods and covered with trees and vineyards. The Höhenstrasse, a scenic route lined with trees that occasionally offers a glimpse of the city, winds its way up the Kahlenberg from Grinzing, and on top of the hill you can enjoy a breathtaking view of the city. During the Turkish siege of 1683, the Polish troops under King Jan III Sobieski descended from the top of this hill and defeated the Turkish army on 12 September that year. The little Baroque church on top of Kahlenberg commemorates this historic event. *Train Nussdorf; Bus 38A*

Kahlenberg

8 Leopoldsberg

Just next to Kahlenberg is its twin mountain, the Leopoldsberg, dominating the Danube valley. From the top of the 425-m (1,400-ft) high mountain, you get an excellent view of the entire region around Vienna. Leopoldsberg is named after the Babenberg ruler Leopold III (1073–1136) and the ruins of the 13th-century Babenberg castle destroyed by the Turks in 1529 are still visible. An older church on top of the mountain was also destroyed by the Turks and was replaced by a Baroque church in the 18th century. *Train Nussdorf; Bus 38A; U-Bahn U4 Heiligenstadt*

9 Geymüllerschlössel

The Geymüllerschlössel is a summer palace off the beaten track, reflecting the Biedermeier style. It is owned by the Museum for Applied Arts and houses a collection of 170 clocks, among them an early Viennese flute clock (c.1800) playing music by Haydn. *Khevenmüllerstrasse 2 • Open May– Nov: 11am–6pm Sat & Sun • Tram 41 then Bus 41A • 711 36 298 • Adm*

10 Heiligenstädter Beethoven House

The composer Ludwig van Beethoven often came to Heiligenstadt to spend his summers – Vienna's bourgeoisie favoured the area as a holiday resort in the late 18th century. Beethoven lived in various houses in Heiligenstadt. In 1802 he stayed at Probusgasse 6 and visited the nearby spa to gain relief for his deafness; when nothing helped, he wrote the Heiligenstädter Testament, a desperate letter to his brothers. Today, the house is a museum. *Probusgasse 6 • U-Bahn U4, U6; Tram D; Bus 38A • Open 10am–1pm, 2–6pm Tue–Sun & hols; closed 1 Jan, 1 May & 25 Dec • Adm*

A Day on Vienna's Outskirts

Morning

To beat the crowds and enjoy the peace, begin your day at the former imperial summer residence **Schloss Schönbrunn** *(see pp36–9)*. You could easily spend a day in the palace, walking in the park and having a look at all the features of the formal French garden, or visiting the world's oldest zoo at Schönbrunn park. For a relaxing coffee or tea, head towards the far end of the park to the coffee house in the Gloriette building. The view of the palace and the city is very rewarding.

Stroll through the park towards the Hietzinger gate of the palace. The Hietzinger Bräu is just around the corner, where you could get the taste of a real *Tafelspitz (see p70)* for lunch.

Afternoon

After lunch, head towards the **Kirche am Steinhof** *(see p123)* by Bus 48A, but take into account that guided tours through the interior only take place on Saturday and Sunday afternoons. Nearby Lainzer Tiergarten, part of the Vienna Woods, with the **Hermesvilla** *(see p123)* is on the U-Bahn U4 line (then a 2-hour walk).

If you favour a more rustic experience, head northwest towards **Kahlenberg** and **Leopoldsberg** with their vineyards and hiking paths.

To bring the day to a cosy conclusion, make your way to **Grinzing** by public transport or taxi to enjoy Viennese vintages in one of the many wine taverns.

Following pages: **Ironwork exterior of the Palm House in Schloss Schönbrunn Gardens**

Left **Vienna International Centre** Right **Nussdorf**

TOP 10 Best of the Rest

1 Schloss Hof
This was the former country seat of Prince Eugene of Savoy and later Empress Maria Theresa. *Imperial Festival Palace Hof • Open Apr–Oct: 10am–6pm daily • www.schlosshof.at*

2 Nussdorf
Nussdorf's picturesque location amid hills overgrown with vineyards is complemented by its long narrow streets. The composer Ludwig van Beethoven spent some time here in 1824. *Train Nussdorf; Tram D*

3 Vienna International Centre
The centre, also known as the UNO City, dominates the skyline. Built in the 1970s, the building is the Vienna headquarters of the United Nations. *Wagramerstrasse 5 • U-Bahn U1 • Guided tours (ID needed) 11am & 2pm Mon–Fri, also 12:30pm in Jul & Aug • Adm • www.unvienna.org*

4 Ernst Fuchs Museum
Otto Wagner built this villa between 1886 and 1888. Today it is owned by Ernst Fuchs, a painter of the Phantastic Realism school. *Hüttelbergstrasse 26 • U-Bahn U4 • Bus 52A, 52B • Open 10am–6pm Tue–Sun & public hols by appt (tel. 01 914 85 75) • Adm • www.ernstfuchsmuseum.at*

5 Lehar-Schikaneder Schlössl
This Baroque palace was home to composer Franz Lehár in the 1930s and Emanuel Schikaneder, who wrote the libretto for Mozart's *The Magic Flute*. *Hackhofergasse 18 • U-Bahn U4 • Tram D • Open by appt (tel. 01 318 5416) • Free*

6 Sankt-Marxer-Friedhof
The St Marx Cemetery is the resting place for prominent Austrians, including Wolfgang Amadeus Mozart, whose actual burial site remains a mystery. *Leberstrasse 6–8 • Bus 74A • Open daily • Free*

7 Lobau
The Lobau is spread over more than 4,900 acres and creates a romantic landscape, with trails winding between lakes and a path with labelled plants and trees. *U-Bahn U1 • Bus 92B, 93A*

8 Laxenburg
The Laxenburg palace and its park were established by Empress Maria Theresa in the 18th century. *U-Bahn U1, then bus from Südtiroler Platz • www.schloss-laxenburg.at*

9 Sammlung Essl
This collection of contemporary art includes works by artists Hermann Nitsch and Maria Lassnig. *An der Donau-Au 1 • U-Bahn U4, bus/train to Klosterneuburg • Open 10am–6pm Tue–Sun (to 9pm Wed) • www.essl.museum.at*

10 Klosterneuburg
This ancient town has a fine Augustine abbey founded in the early 12th century by the Babenberg ruler Leopold III. *U-Bahn U4; Bus 238, 239; Train Klosterneuburg*

Price Categories

For a three-course meal for one with half a bottle of wine (or equivalent meal), taxes and extra charges.	
€	under €25
€€	€25–€35
€€€	€35–€55
€€€€	€55–€70
€€€€€	over €70

Above **Café Dommayer**

Top 10 Places to Eat

1 Mraz & Sohn
This restaurant is simply one of the best in Vienna. The chef's innovative cooking can be enjoyed in a relaxed and inviting setting. *Wallensteinstrasse 59 • Tram 5, 33 • 01 330 45 94 • Dis. access • €€€€€*

2 Café Dommayer
A traditional café with red velvet upholstery, a wooden veranda and a pretty garden. Johann Strauss used to give concerts here. *Johann-Strauss-Platz/ Auhofstrasse 2 • U-Bahn U4 • 01 877 54 65 • Dis. access • €€*

3 Meixner's Gastwirtschaft
Located in a Viennese suburb, family-owned Meixner's prepares Viennese cuisine at the highest level. Be sure to sample the Austrian lamb and Austrian artisan beer. *Buchengasse 64 • U-Bahn U1 • 01 604 27 10 • Closed Mon • Dis. access • €€*

4 Fischerbräu
The old wooden interior of this restaurant and pub with its own brewery has a great atmosphere. The beer garden is pleasant in summer. *Billrothstrasse 17 • U-Bahn U6 • Tram 37, 38 • 01 369 59 49 • No credit cards • Dis. access • €€*

5 Café-Restaurant Lusthaus
The pavilion in the middle of the Prater park was built in 1874 as a meeting point for the imperial hunting party (now a restaurant). *Freudenau 254, end of Prater Hauptallee • Bus 77A • 01 728 95 65 • €€€*

6 La Creperie
On the banks of the Danube, this is perfect for a romantic summer evening. Pick a table or have a candlelit dinner on a boat. *An der Oberen Alten Donau 6 • U-Bahn U6 • 01 270 31 00 • Dis. access • €€€*

7 Grünspan
Wooden floors and a rustic design give this spacious beer hall an inviting atmosphere. Traditional food is served with finesse. *Ottakringer Strasse 266 • U-Bahn U3; Bus 45B, 46B; Tram 46 • 01 480 57 30 • No credit cards • Dis. access • €€€*

8 Hadikstüberl
A genuine Viennese restaurant with a rustic and cosy interior. Dishes vary with the seasons. *Hadikgasse 100 • U-Bahn U4 • 01 894 63 21 • Closed Sat & Sun eve • No credit cards • Dis. access • €€*

9 Villa Aurora
In a spectacular location overlooking the city, Villa Aurora serves inventive *Schnitzel* creations and tasty vegetarian dishes. There is a garden for picnics. *Wilhelminenstrasse 237 • Bus 146 • 01 489 33 33 • No credit cards • Dis. access • €€€*

10 Tempel
Located near the house where "The Blue Danube Waltz" was penned, Tempel offers a variety of dishes. *Praterstrasse 56, inner courtyard • Map B6 • U-Bahn Nestroyplatz • 01 214 01 79 • Closed for lunch Sat, Sun, Mon • Dis. access • €€€*

***Note:** Unless otherwise stated, all restaurants accept credit cards and serve vegetarian meals*

STREETSMART

Left **Airport Wien Schwechat transit area** Right **Airport Wien Schwechat**

Top 10 Getting to Vienna

1 Arriving by Plane

Most European airlines offer services to the Austrian capital. Austrian carriers Lauda Air, Tyrolean Airways and Austrian Airlines offer flights from Europe and the US. *Tickets 01 51789 • General Information: www.aua.com • www.viennaairport.com*

2 Airport Wien Schwechat

Vienna's international airport is 20 km (12.5 miles) southeast of the city. Taxis to the centre cost about €36; the airport bus costs €8. A commuter train on the S7 line also operates between 5am and 11pm and is a cheaper option at €4. The CAT (City Airport Train) runs every 30 minutes from Terminal Wien Mitte and costs €11.

3 Arriving by Rail

Vienna has several main railway lines that link up to most major European destinations. Details of train times can be obtained from Austrian Federal Railways, the ÖBB. *ÖBB: 01 51717 • www.oebb.at*

4 Railway Stations

This is a time of change for Vienna's main city rail termini as international arrivals and departures are gradually transferred to the new Hauptbahnhof, on the site of the old Südbahnhof. Some international services may continue to use Vienna's Meidling and Westbahnhof stations until the Hauptbahnhof is fully operational. All three termini – Hauptbahnhof, Meidling and Westbahnhof – are interconnected by city public transport. *• www.oebb.at • www.hauptbahn-wien.at*

5 Arriving by Coach

Coach (long-distance bus) services are often the cheapest way to reach Vienna, although not the quickest or most comfortable. Most services, including Eurolines, operate from the Vienna International Bus Terminal, Edberg. The Austrian ÖBB bus service has excellent links with the rest of the country. *Eurolines: 01 798 29 00 • www.eurolines.at*

6 Arriving by Boat

Vienna is accessible by high-speed hydrofoil or ship from a number of cities along the Danube, including Bratislava (Slovakia), Budapest (Hungary) and Passau (Germany). *DDSG Blue Danube Schiffahrt GmbH • 01 588 80 0 • www.ddsg-blue-danube.at*

7 Arriving by Car

If you are visiting from Germany or Switzerland, you will arrive on the Westautobahn (A1). Drivers coming from the south will arrive on the Südautobahn (A2). A toll sticker is needed on all Austrian motorways, and is purchased when entering the country.

8 Parking

In Vienna, districts 1st–9th and 20th are short-term parking areas for which special tickets are required. With these tickets you can park for 90 minutes from 9am until 10pm Monday to Friday in the 1st district and elsewhere for 120 minutes. But beware of special signs and different times in shopping areas. Ticket prices range from €1 to €4 and can be bought from newsagents, some banks, railway stations and at most public transport ticket offices. Disabled people can park for free. Hotels in short-term parking areas offer free tickets to guests.

9 Passports and Visas

All visitors travelling to Austria need a valid passport or form of ID. Some non-EU residents may require a visa – for more information, contact your Austrian embassy before leaving home.

10 Customs

For EU travellers, there are no restrictions on importing cigarettes, spirits and perfume. From outside the EU, you can import duty-free 200 cigarettes or equivalent, spirits up to 2 litres, 50 g of perfume, and up to €175 in other goods.

***Note:** The German word for street is* Strasse*, which you may also see written on road signs as* Straße

Left **Vienna bus** Centre **Tram stop** Right **Vienna taxi**

TOP 10 Getting Around Vienna

1 Underground

There are five underground lines in Vienna, distinguished by colour and number, connecting all parts of the city. It is a fast, clean and reliable way of getting around. A single ticket valid on bus, tram, underground and special S-Bahn (Fast Trains) costs €2.20 (€2.30 if you buy it on board). You need to buy reduced (€1.20) tickets for children, dogs and bikes. You can also buy tickets valid for 24 hours (€7.60), 48 hours (€13.30) or 72 hours (€16.30). They can be bought at underground stations and newsagents.

2 Trams

Vienna's first trams, which were horse-drawn, started in 1865. Since then the Viennese have feverishly expanded this network. Trams clearly show their destination at the front of the vehicle and tickets can be bought from machines at the front of the tram. Ticket prices are the same as for the underground.

3 Buses

There are about 60 bus lines to choose from, and this is the only public transport operating in the 1st district, as well as some suburbs. Tickets are purchased on board the bus from the driver. All buses have machines on board for you to validate your ticket with a stamp.

4 Trains

The S-Bahn (Fast Train) is an important rail service within the city, especially along the north–southwest trunk line or the S7 to the airport. The normal public transport tickets used for bus, tram and underground travel are valid on S-Bahn trains within Vienna city limits. All three major S-Bahn stations are accessible by public transport.

5 Fiakers

If you prefer a more leisurely way of getting around Vienna, the best would be in a horse-drawn cab known as a *Fiaker*. Once Vienna's taxi transport, today they are mostly used for ceremonial purposes and as a tourist attraction. *Fiaker* ranks are at the Staatsoper, the Hofburg Complex and beside the Stephansdom Cathedral.

6 Cycling

A bicycle is an ideal way to explore Vienna. A free bike service known as ViennaBike is currently in operation and guided tours by bike are also available. *Cycle information: www.info.wien.at • www.pedalpower.at*

7 Taxis

Vienna's taxis are numerous, although most prefer to collect passengers at the ranks or by prebooking rather than being flagged down. Taxis are run by reputable companies and cases of abuse are rare. The minimum charge is €3.80 during the day, followed by an extra €0.20 per kilometre. The minimum charge at night, Sundays and holidays is €4.30.

8 Boat

The boarding station for most boat trips on the Danube is at Schwedenplatz (U1,U4), which is on a tributary, or on the river itself at the Reichsbrücke.

9 Driving

When driving in Vienna you will need to carry a valid international driving licence at all times, as well as a toll sticker *(vignette)* for the motorways and A roads *(see entry 7 opposite)*. Speed limits on motorways are 130 km/h (80 km/h), 100 km/h (60 mph) on country roads and 50 km/h (30 mph) in towns and villages.

10 Walking

Compared to many scrawling metropolises, Vienna's compact size means it is often best seen on foot. Since many of Vienna's important attractions are within the Ringstrasse, distances are not great. Walking Vienna's old town district is also a great way to discover little side streets and other easily missed hidden places.

The U-Bahn runs for 24 hours at weekends, from Friday to Sunday evening

Left **Tourist Information sign** Right **Newspaper stand**

Top 10 Information and Tours

1 Austrian Tourist Office

The Austrian Tourist Office can provide you with general information. Questions concerning travel tips, accommodation, culture, weather reports and more will be answered by the helpful staff by telephone or email 9am–5pm Mon–Fri. *Austria: 0800 400 200 00 (toll free); Great Britain: 0845 101 18 18; USA: 212 944 6880 • travel@austria.info • www.austria.info*

2 Vienna Tourist Office

At the Vienna Tourist Office you can pick up leaflets on the city's sights and cultural events as well as on accommodation and guided tours. *Albertinaplatz/ Maysedergasse • Map M5 • 01 24 555 • Open 9am–7pm daily • www.wien.info*

3 Websites

For general information visit www.austria-tourism.at. The website of the Vienna Tourist Board also contains information for blind visitors (www.info.wien.at). Other useful websites are given below. *www.magwien.gv.at/english • www.welcome-vienna.com • www.virtualvienna.net*

4 Falter

Falter, die Wiener Stadtzeitung (the Vienna City Newspaper) gives an excellent and comprehensive insight of what's going on in Vienna. It is available at any newsagent. Even if you don't speak German, the listings are easy to follow.

5 Wien-Programm

The monthly brochure *Wien-Programm* offers an excellent overview of what Vienna has to offer. The listings include virtually every event in the city, ranging from festivals to concerts, from theatre and opera performances to sport events and markets. You can pick it up for free in travel agencies, tourist offices and ticket offices.

6 English-Language Newspapers

There is only one English-language newspaper, *Austria Today*, which is also on the Internet (www.austriatoday.at) *(see p136)*.

7 Walking Tours

If you want to explore Vienna on foot you can join a variety of topical guided tours. Choose to follow in the footsteps of Mozart, Beethoven and Schubert, take a tour through the old city or Jewish Vienna or descend to underground Vienna *(see pp62–3)*. *Vienna Walks & Talks: 01 774 89 01; www.vienna-walks.com • Wiener Spaziergänge: 01 489 96 74; www.wienguide.at • Verliebt in Wien: 01 889 28 06; www.verliebtinwien.at • PerPedes: 01 544 96 68; www.perpedes.at • City Segway Tours: 01 712 46 83 80 • www.viennaguideservice.at*

8 Bus Tours

Several companies run bus tours to Vienna's most famous sights. As in many European cities there is also a hop-on-, hop-off bus circling the most famous landmarks, allowing you enough time to stay at whichever sight you like most. *Vienna Sightseeing Tours: 01 712 46 830, www.viennasightseeingtours.com • Hop On Hop Off: 01 712 46 83 • Red Bus City Tours: 01 512 40 30, www.redbuscitytours.at • Cityrama: 01 504 75 00, www.cityrama.at*

9 Cycling Tours

Exploring Vienna on a bike is a good way to see the sights from a relaxed perspective. Pedal Power offers guided bike tours of two to three hours in spring and summer. *01 729 72 34 • www pedalpower.at*

10 Boat Tours

Boat trips regularly head off from Vienna along the Wachau Valley. Alternatively, trips the other way head to Bratislava (1 hour) and Budapest (4 hours). All ships have restaurants and sundecks. Themed cruises are also available. *www.ddsg-blue-danube.at*

There is also a branch of the Vienna Tourist Office at Schwechat International Airport, opposite the baggage carousels

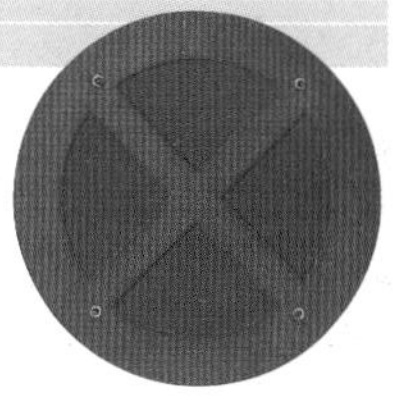

Left **Leisurely coffee break** Right **No Parking sign**

TOP 10 Things to Avoid

1 Public Transport Fines

Many visitors get caught by the ticket inspector for failing to validate their ticket by putting it into the slot at one of the blue machines at the entrances to underground stations or on buses or trams. Fines for first-time offenders are as much as €150.

2 Bad Parking

Although the tow-away system is not the best in Europe, the Viennese are fast to do their civic duty and report anyone blocking driveways. If your car is seized or caught in a clamp after a short but illegal stay, the police are the first port of call. Make sure you have the registration and street address to hand.

3 Vienna Black Spots

Vienna increasingly is suffering the same problems of street crime experienced in all major cities. In addition to the usual precautions, the Prater theme park should be avoided in winter when it is deserted. Visitors shouldn't linger in certain underground stations, such as Meidling and Praterstern, for longer than it takes to get on and off the train.

4 Forgetting to Tip

Tipping in Austria is a way of showing that you were happy with the service and is not included in the price. Saying thank you *(Danke)* when handing over the cash means "keep the change". A good rule of thumb is to tip 10 per cent of the total bill. A smaller tip is acceptable, but no tip means the service was bad and is seen as a way of complaining.

5 Queues

Viennese have no concept of how to behave in a queue so the "everyone for themselves" rule applies. Particularly annoying are banks and post offices where it's hit-and-miss whether you join the right queue and don't get stuck behind someone arguing for the next hour.

6 Regulations

The Viennese frown on petty lawbreakers as though they were major criminals. They follow the most little-known rules such as "don't walk on the grass" even when walking home drunk in the early hours of the morning. Crossing on a red light will risk a fine even if there's not a car in sight. Older Viennese are often seen chastising others for anything from walking on the grass to making too much noise.

7 Coffee in a Hurry

The traditional coffee shops in Vienna are famous for their grumpy and usually slow waiters. This is a part of the city's charm, but if you are in a hurry pay when the drink or snack turns up or else expect a long wait. Most bakery chains like Anker and Ströck serve coffee on the go. Also there are several branches of Starbucks in the city.

8 Credit Cards

Don't expect to be able to use your credit cards as easily as back home. Some restaurants and small shops don't regard the number of credit cards used worth the investment in the equipment. Check if you can use your card before running up a large bill.

9 Shopping on a Sunday

Sunday is still seen as a holy day in Catholic Austria, and most shops stay closed. Most bakeries are granted exemption and stay open until noon. There are supermarkets open at Hauptbahnhof Wien, Westbahnhof and Wien Nord stations. Shops at larger petrol stations are also open.

10 Bureaucracy

Countless forms and official applications need to be filled out before achieving anything, from obtaining a yearly ticket for the underground to filing a complaint with an official body. This creates long waiting times and can be very tiring.

Left & Centre left **Automatic exchange machines** Centre right **Post office sign** Right **Telephone**

Top 10 Banking and Communications

1 Currency
Since 1 January 2002 the official currency used in Austria is the euro, which replaced the old Austrian currency, the schilling. Euro banknotes have the following denominations: 5, 10, 20, 50, 100, 200 and 500. Euro coins come in eight denominations: 1 euro, 2 euros, and 1, 2, 5, 10, 20 and 50 cents. Visitors from outside the euro zone should check the exchange rates at the time of travel. Notes and coins can be used regardless of origin throughout the euro zone.

2 Credit Cards
Not as widely used as in other places. Check signs on the door before running up a high bill *(see p135)*.

3 Cash Dispensers
Cash dispensers can be found all over Vienna, usually next to banks. You can easily spot them by the sign mounted above or near the cash dispenser that resembles a letter "B" in blue and green. It is also possible to pay with debit cards in most of the shops and restaurants.

4 Changing Money
You can change money at banks, at the usual bureaux de change all around the city, or at one of the automated changing machines in the city centre.

5 Post Offices
Yellow-fronted post offices are usually open 8am–noon and 2–6pm Monday to Friday. District post offices remain open during lunch hours and are open 8–10am on Saturdays. Post offices in railway stations and the main post office (Fleischmarkt 19) are open 24 hours daily.

6 Public Telephones
Public coin-box (booth) telephones are are gradually being phased out due to lack of demand. The remaining phone booths are coin-operated. If you would like to make an international call without using your mobile phone, most post offices offer this service. The international dialling code for Austria is 0043 and 01 for Vienna.

7 Internet Cafés
Vienna offers a wide range of Internet cafés and you will be able to find terminals in many coffee houses and pubs. These include BigNet branches at Kärntner Strasse 61 in the 1st district (open 10am–2am daily) and at Mariahilfer Strasse 27 in the 6th district (open 8am–2am daily), with more than 200 workstations.

8 Mobile Phones
Austria has a widely developed mobile phone network, and even phones from abroad will work all over the city and on the underground – as long as the roaming function has been cleared. It is possible to buy chip cards, which can be charged with a set value for the duration of your holiday.

9 Newspapers and Magazines
Most publications in Austria are state-subsidized and as a result usually follow the same agenda even though they have different party affiliations. The largest is the tabloid *Kronen Zeitung* and its upmarket sister the *Kurier*. *Die Presse* is the most respected and *Der Standard* is the best business paper. Larger newsstands will sell international papers such as the *International New York Times* and the *Times*, *The Economist*, and the *Guardian*, usually one day after publication. *Falter* is the main listings magazine *(see p134)*.

10 Television and Radio
Austrian TV has three state channels (ORF 1, ORF 2 and ORF III) and several private channels, such as ATV, Servus TV and Puls 4. Most hotels have satellite channels. The radio station FM4 is broadcast on 103.8 with news in English, German and French. Also Ö1 on 91.9 has news in English and French on weekdays at 12:50pm.

Left **Vienna police car** Right **Vienna pharmacy**

Top 10 Security and Health

1 Crime

Vienna was one of the safest cities in Europe, but unfortunately crime levels have risen. Travelling by public transport poses few dangers, and police are omnipresent in case of trouble *(see p135)*.

2 Police

Emergency numbers can be called for free from any landline, mobile or phone booth. You will have to give your name, the address of the emergency and how many people are involved. Police stations are located all across Vienna and you should report any crime.

3 Pickpockets

Pickpocketing is probably the most common crime you may face in Vienna. As a tourist you are a potential target at queues and busy places (particularly at cash dispensers). It is also quite common on the underground. Stay alert, keep credit cards in a different place to your money and bags closed.

4 Public Transport

Fast, efficient and clean, Vienna's public transport is a model for the world, in part because it is heavily funded by the state. Trains, buses, trams and the underground are very secure, but the usual safety precautions should still be applied.

5 Health Care Standards

Austria has one of the finest health care systems in Europe. No expense is spared to give patients first-class medical treatment and, if you have to go to an Austrian doctor or hospital, you can expect a service at least equal in quality to one you might expect at home. Waiting times in surgeries and emergency rooms are also surprisingly small in comparison with other countries.

6 Insurance

Visitors from EU countries will need a European Health Insurance Card (EHIC), available from post offices, to qualify for free or low-cost emergency medical treatment. This is not a substitute for private medical insurance. Non-EU visitors should buy travel insurance to cover medical emergencies.

7 Hospitals

Expect VIP treatment at Austrian hospitals, at least as far as medical care is concerned. Most complaints, if any, centre around the food, so if you are visiting anyone in hospital, food parcels are a good idea.

8 Ambulances

Several organizations run ambulance services across Vienna. If you need an ambulance, call 144, free from any phone.

9 Pharmacies

Addresses of pharmacies *(Apotheken)* can be found in the telephone directory or by calling the emergency chemists' service (recorded information in German) on 01 1550. You can identify pharmacies by the green cross and red "A" outside.

10 Dentists

Besides the usual consulting hours, dentists offer night and weekend services. In cases of emergency, call 01 512 20 78 for further details and you will get recorded information.

Emergency Numbers

Police: 133

Ambulance: 144

Fire: 122

ÖAMTC (for automobile emergencies): 120

Emergency doctor service (nights and weekends): 141

Night and weekend dental service (recorded information): 01 512 20 78

Emergency chemists' service (recorded information): 1550

Pastoral advice service: 1770

Befrienders (in English): 01 713 33 74

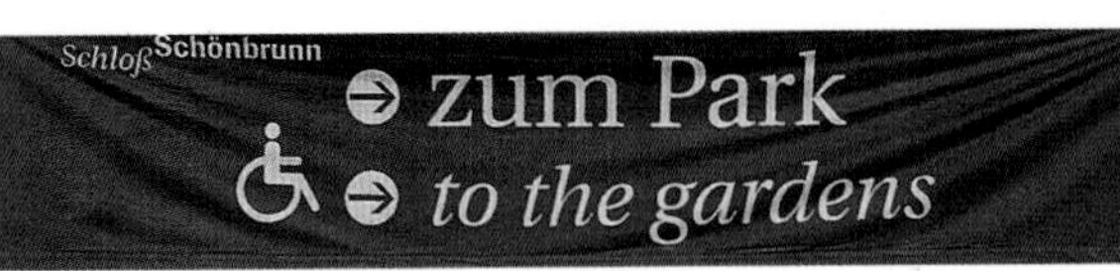

Above **Disabled entrance sign to Schloss Schönbrunn**

Top 10 Tips for the Disabled

1 Tourist Information Office

For your stay in Vienna the Tourist Information Office on Albertinaplatz in the 1st district has a number of booklets for the disabled and offers a disabled booking service. It is open daily 9am–7pm. *Tourist Information Office: 01 24 55 5 • public.rel@info.wien.at*

2 Useful Organizations

Several organizations in Vienna offer help and advice. You can contact Bizeps, an advice centre for people with disabilities, the Austrian Association for the Hearing Impaired and the Austrian Blind Union. *Bizeps: 01 523 8921; www.bizeps.or.at • Austrian Association for the Hearing Impaired: 01 603 08 53; www.oeglb.at • Austrian Blind Union: 01 982 7584-0; www.oebsv.at*

3 Hotels

It is advisable to check before booking accommodation, as many older hotels lack facilities for the disabled. The Vienna Tourist Board has nominated hotels suitable for people with disabilities, among them the ANA Grand Hotel, the Marriott and the Ibis.

4 Taxis

There are a number of taxi and transport companies providing special services. To order a taxi for people with hearing or other disabilities, fax the radio taxi service "40 100" on 918 18 848. The special order form and confirmation will be sent back to you immediately. *Special taxi services: www.info.wien.at*

5 Buses and Trams

Many of the city's public buses have been replaced with street-level vehicles and all buses also now have fold-out ramps. Many tram lines have street-level trams; stops have a blinking wheelchair symbol indicating how many minutes remain before a low-floor tram is due.

6 Underground and Trains

Viennese underground stations are equipped with "guiding stripes" that guide the way to exits, elevators and escalators. A Braille station map of Vienna's underground system can be purchased from the public transport operator Wiener Linien. *Wiener Linien: 01 7909-0*

7 Restaurants

Many restaurants in Vienna are accessible by wheelchair and offer special parking facilities, and some restaurants also offer menus for the visually impaired. Restaurants in historic buildings may not be accessible. It is recommended to call the restaurant prior to the visit to ensure it offers the facilities needed.

8 Attractions

Many of Vienna's attractions are housed in historic buildings and therefore access can be difficult at times. Search the Vienna Tourist Board website (www.wien.info) to find the sights that offer the best services for the disabled.

9 Guided Tours

Several specialized city guides offer tours around Vienna (in various languages) for visitors with special needs. Their contact details can be found on the Vienna Tourist Board website (www.wien.info).

10 Useful Websites

There are several websites that help make your stay in Vienna easier and more enjoyable. www.you-too.net informs about the accessibility of public places in Vienna. www.bizeps.or.at/shop/dolmet.doc offers a list of Austrian sign-language interpreters. Wheelchairs can be rented from the firm Bständig, which has branches all across the city – telephone 01 533 73 04 for details. A useful web address for the impaired of hearing is www.taubenschlag.de/oesterreich. Although both sites are in German they offer various contact numbers of organizations that can help you, where you will find information in English and some other languages.

Left **Reading newspapers in a café** Right **Student information office**

Top 10 Budget Tips in Vienna

1 Public Transport

There are public transport tickets for 72 hours (€16.30) or 24 hours (€7.60), as well as a ticket that allows you to travel on public transport from 8am until 8pm (*Einkaufskarte*, €6.10). Single tickets are better value if you don't plan to use public transport often. Buying tickets at a newsagent or at ticket machines in the underground is also a little cheaper.

2 Vienna Card

This card is a ticket for public transport in combination with reductions at 210 museums, sights, concert venues, theatres, shops, restaurants, cafés and *Heurigen* (wine taverns). For €21.90 you can travel on Vienna's underground, buses, trains and trams for 72 hours. The Vienna Card is available at hotels and tourist offices and from Karlsplatz, Stephansplatz, Wien Mitte, Hauptbahnhof Wien, Westbahnhof and Wien Nord stations.

3 Hostels and B&Bs

There are several youth hostels in Vienna, and some student halls of residence are used as hotels in the summer. A room or an apartment in private homes for a stay of three days or more can be arranged via a private accommodation agency.

Private Accommodation Agency: Westbahnstrasse 19 • 01 402 6061

4 Camping

Bringing your own tent or campervan and staying at one of the four camping sites in Vienna certainly cuts down accommodation costs. Don't attempt this in winter, however – temperatures reach far below zero. For further information, see www.wiencamping.at.

5 Choosing an Area

If you have a small travel budget, it does help to pick the right area for a bite to eat and accommodation. Central Vienna can get pretty expensive, but staying in a hotel or a B&B a bit further afield reduces the costs considerably.

6 Newspapers

Although traditional Viennese cafés might be expensive, you will never be told to leave when you have finished your cup of coffee. You can sip your *Melange* *(see p77)* and your glass of water for hours, while having the choice of reading a range of daily national and international newspapers and magazines.

7 Cheap Theatre Seats

Vienna's theatres and concert halls offer a superb programme and are also affordable for small budgets. There are reduced prices for children under 15, for students and people doing army or community service. Thirty minutes before any performance, the remaining tickets are sold at a cheaper price, and on producing a valid student ID they cost even less. For between €1.20 and €2 you can get standing tickets for a performance in the Burgtheater or the Staatsoper.

8 Cheap Cinema Seats

Cinema Monday means all seats are the same price (€5.40), regardless of where you sit, following the first-come-first-served principle. But many cinemas also offer reduced prices on other days of the week.

9 Cheap Eats

Although eating out in Vienna can be expensive, there is a wide range of reasonably priced restaurants, and a midday set menu, on offer in most places, is always a bargain. Avoid eateries along the tourist trails and go for traditional Viennese places, particularly around the university and the Town Hall and Museumsquartier.

10 Concessions

Vienna's sights have high admission fees, but most offer reduced fees to students with ID, to pensioners and to families. Some sights and museums have one day a week where entrance fees are reduced or free.

On the Austrian national holiday, every 26 October, entrance to all museums is free

Left **Sachertorte cake packaging** Right **Food and wine stall**

TOP 10 Shopping Tips

1 What to Buy
Vienna's best buys are all kinds of chocolates as well as cakes and pastries, with the Sachertorte being the most famous *(see pp72–3)*. High-quality ground coffees are offered throughout the city. You will also find beautiful glassware and porcelain in traditional patterns, such as Augarten, but the exclusive items tend to be quite expensive. Other Austrian goods are coats and jackets made of the woollen fabric Loden, as well as traditional clothing such as Dirndl dresses.

2 Opening Hours
Vienna's shops are, with a few exceptions, closed on Sundays and public holidays. Generally shops are open from around 8am or 9am to around 6pm. Smaller shops close for an hour at lunchtime, and on Saturdays shops close at 5pm. Supermarkets at main train stations and large petrol stations are open seven days a week.

3 How to Pay
Paying by cash is still the preferred method in some restaurants and bars, but almost all shops, particularly large stores, have ATM machines and will accept debit cards and major credit cards – but always check this in advance just to be sure.

4 Taxes
As a foreign visitor to Vienna (and non-EU resident) you are entitled to a VAT/GST refund on purchases. Look out for the Global Refund Tax Free Shopping stickers in shop windows or ask the shop assistant for details. The VAT (value-added tax) in Austria is 20 per cent.

5 Where to Shop
The shopping streets in the 1st district around the Kärntner Strasse, Graben and Kohlmarkt area *(see p92)* are great, if pricey. Mariahilfer Strasse *(see p110)* is the less expensive option. Kärntner Strasse also has cheaper clothing stores such as H&M and Esprit. There are several large shopping centres within the city, such as The Mall at Wien Mitte station and Bahnhof-City Wien West at Westbahnhof station as well as the Donauzentrum (U1 line to Kagran) and the Stadion Center (U2 line to Stadion).

6 Gifts
Vienna's best gifts are chocolates in pretty boxes, such as the world-famous Mozart balls or the *Sisi Taler*. Many *Konditoreien* (cake shops) offer Sachertorte packed in a wooden case to take home; some will also ship them for you across the globe. Bottles of Austrian wine or Schnapps also make nice gifts. Vienna's museum shops have a range of beautiful items.

7 Food and Drink
In addition to chocolates, there are many delicatessen shops that sell jars of jam, pickled vegetables, Austrian wines and other goodies. The best food shopping area for nibbles from Asia to Eastern Europe is Naschmarkt *(see p109)*. Be it spices, special vinegars, sweets or cheese, you will find something to your taste.

8 Music and Books
There are several bookstores in Vienna that specialize in English literature and you will find a few bestsellers in large bookshop. For music try the EMI Music Store on Kärntnerstrasse or Gramola on Graben.

9 Jewellery
Viennese jewellery is world-famous. Köchert and Heldwein were the jewellers at the imperial court and the company still makes pieces in their workshops on Neuer Markt and Graben. Frey Wille and Österreichische Werkstätten offer an Art Nouveau-inspired collection.

10 Clothes
International designer shops are situated in the city centre. Austria's international fashion export, Helmut Lang, runs a flagship store on Seilergasse. Labels specializing in traditional Austrian clothes are Gössl, Geiger and Giesswein.

Left **Typical Heuriger** Centre **Viennese cake** Right **Sausage stand**

TOP 10 Eating & Accommodation Tips

1 What to Eat

Viennese cuisine was influenced by the food from the Habsburg lands in imperial times, notably Bohemia. It picked the best dishes from each country and developed them to Viennese taste buds. Although the Viennese love hearty and rather heavy meat dishes, most restaurants also offer vegetarian dishes. Between meals, don't miss the enormous variety of cakes and pastries accompanied by a cup of coffee.

2 Types of Restaurants

Throughout the city you can find all types of restaurants ranging from elegant eateries to *Beisl* – traditional Viennese places serving simple dishes. But Vienna is most famous for its coffee houses that are cosy, unhurried places where time seems to stand still. The *Heurigen* (wine taverns) serve hearty food and local wine *(see pp74–5)*. *Würstelstände* are little sausage stalls scattered all around town and open late in the evenings.

3 Dress Codes

When going out in Vienna you can dress quite casually most of the time, but the grand restaurants and stylish bars in the city centre expect their customers to dress smartly.

4 Reservations

It is advisable to make reservations if you are planning to eat at a special restaurant. Restaurants in the city centre can get very busy – if you are in a big group, make sure you book a table. Except for luxury restaurants and some bars, you may choose your own table and don't need to wait to be seated.

5 How Much to Pay

The variety of restaurants mirrors the variation in prices. A meal at a coffee shop (including coffee) might cost you about €12, but in a *Beisl* you may pay only €2.80 for a soup and €6–€14 for a main course. Meals at luxury restaurants start at about €18. Most places offer a bargain midday set menu for a two- or three-course meal for between €7 and €12.

6 Types of Accommodation

Vienna's hotels range from 1- to 5-star and the most luxurious are in the city centre. The cheaper options are B&Bs, called *Pensionen*, where you usually get good service for your money. There are various youth hostels in town and students' halls of residence are rented out during the summer. There are four camping sites around Vienna *(see p139)*.

7 Which Areas to Choose

The area in which you pick a hotel inevitably influences the price. Vienna's 1st district is the most expensive, although alongside the posh hotels there are also several B&Bs. The Town Hall and Museums-quartier is very popular with budget travellers.

8 Hotel Prices

Most hotels and *Pensionen* have rooms at various rates depending on the size and the facilities. Single rooms are usually three-quarters of the price of double rooms. Vienna's low season runs from November to March, but only some hotels drop their prices at that time.

9 Booking

If you are visiting Vienna in peak season (April to October), book in advance. Verify the time of day you will arrive, so that you do not find your room rented out to someone else. The Vienna Tourist Office *(see p134)* offers help with bookings.

10 Hidden Extras

Accommodation prices usually include a Continental breakfast in B&Bs and a buffet in some hotels. Drinks from the minibar will always cost extra, as well as making phone calls from your room. VAT is included in the hotel prices.

Left **Hotel Sacher** Right **Marriott Vienna**

Top 10 Luxury Hotels

1 Hotel Sacher

Ever since the Hotel Sacher was founded in 1876 it has been a Viennese institution, with guests ranging from emperors, diplomats and artists. At the adjoining café, writers such as Arthur Schnitzler used to enjoy a piece of the famous Sachertorte with a coffee. The hotel still ranks among Vienna's most luxurious. All rooms are individually furnished. *Philharmonikerstrasse 4 • Map M5 • 01 514 56 • www.sacher.com • Dis. access • €€€€€*

2 Palais Coburg Hotel Residenz

This luxurious hotel is housed in a 19th-century historic building. There are in-house health and beauty facilities, as well as the Coburg spa on the top floor, which offers good views. *Coburgbastei 4 • Map P4 • 01 518 18 0 • www.palais-coburg.com • Dis. access • €€€€€*

3 Hotel Bristol

One of the top addresses in town, Hotel Bristol is where celebrities and politicians often stay for official or private visits. The 140 rooms offer great views of the Staatsoper opposite. The hotel provides all sorts of thoughtful treats, such as umbrellas for rainy days. *Kärntner Ring 1 • Map N6 • 01 515 160 • www.bristolvienna.com • Dis. access • €€€€€*

4 Imperial

This hotel, rich in tradition, opened in 1873 and soon turned into a meeting place for Austro-Hungarian nobility. Today it still has a grand flair. Delights from the hotel's confectioners include the *Imperialtorte*, created for the hotel's opening to honour Emperor Franz Joseph I. *Kärntner Ring 16 • Map N6 • 01 501 100 • www.imperialvienna.com • Dis. access • €€€€€*

5 Vienna Intercontinental

Although the hotel is housed in a very modern building, this is one of Vienna's luxurious 5-star hotels. It is located opposite the Stadtpark and just a stone's throw from the Konzerthaus. The interior offers 453 plush rooms that guarantee a pleasant stay. *Johannesgasse 28 • Map Q6 • 01 711 220 • www.intercontinental.com/Vienna • Dis. access • €€€€€*

6 Das Triest

This chic boutique hotel is within walking distance of most major sights. The rooms, some with their own terrace or private garden, are individually furnished and feature works by local and international artists. *Wiedner Hauptstrasse 12 • Map F4 • 01 589 18 • www.dastriest.at • €€€€€*

7 Marriott Vienna

The Marriott is within walking distance of all the famous landmarks. It has an indoor swimming pool and a health club where you can relax after a day's sightseeing. *Parkring 12a • Map P5 • 01 515 180 • www.viennamarriott.at • Dis. access • €€€€€*

8 Hotel de France

Built in 1872, this hotel still has an elegant flair combined with all modern comforts. There are conference and banqueting halls and three restaurants. *Schottenring 3 • Map L1 • 01 313 680 • www.hoteldefrance.at • Dis. access • €€€€€*

9 Renaissance Wien Hotel

This modern hotel with a rooftop pool is situated near Schloss Schönbrunn and 10 minutes on the underground from the city centre. *Linke Wienzeile/Ullmanstrasse 71 • U-Bahn U4 • 01 891 02 • www.renaissancewien.at • Dis. access • €€€€*

10 Radisson Blu Palais Hotel Vienna

The Palais Leitenberger and the Palais Henckel von Donnersmarck were converted into this 5-star hotel in the late 20th century. The hotel has non-smoking and anti-allergy rooms. *Parkring 16 • Map P5 • 01 515 170 • www.radissonblu.com/palaishotel-vienna • Dis. access • €€€€€*

***Note:** Unless otherwise stated, all hotels accept credit cards, have en-suite bathrooms and air conditioning*

Price Categories

For a standard, double room per night (with breakfast if included), taxes and extra charges.

€	under €80
€€	€80–€150
€€€	€150–€200
€€€€	€200–€280
€€€€€	over €280

Above **Hotel Regina**

Top 10 Hotels in Great Locations

1 Grand Hotel Wien

Opened in 1870, this hotel is housed in one of the elegant mansions along the Ringstrasse and has an early 20th-century feel. Its 250 spacious, luxurious rooms and suites are decorated in Art Nouveau style. *Kärntner Ring 9 • Map N6 • 01 515 800 • www.grandhotelwien.com • Dis. access • €€€€€*

2 Hotel Park-Villa

This hotel is situated in the elegant Döbling neighbourhood. It was where well-off Viennese once spent their summers. Hotel Park-Villa is located in a magnificent villa and has a terrace leading into the garden. Most of the rooms have balconies. *Hasenauerstrasse 12 • Bus 40A • 01 367 5700 • www.parkvilla.at • Dis. access • €€€*

3 Hotel Schloss Wilhelminenberg

Count Lascy, an Austrian aristocrat, had this palace built between 1781 and 1784 on his hunting grounds. The hotel is situated on top of the Wilhelminen mountain in a large park and offers a wonderful view of Vienna. Well located, it only takes about 30 minutes to get here from the city centre. *Savoyenstrasse 2 • Bus 146B • 01 485 85030 • www.austria-trend.at • Dis. access • No air conditioning • €€€€*

4 Das Opernring

This hotel in the grand Historicist style of the Ringstrasse is located opposite the Staatsoper. The rooms' balconies overlook the tree-lined Ring and offer a wonderful view of some of the buildings along the boulevard. *Opernring 11 • Map M5 • 01 587 5518 • www.opernring.at • Dis. access • No air conditioning • €€€€*

5 The Ring

Located directly on the Ring, just a stone's throw away from the State Opera House and main shopping district, the rooms at this boutique hotel are sumptuously decorated in a contemporary style. Guests can relax in the well-equipped fitness room, sauna, steam bath or full-service spa. *Kärntner Ring 8 • Map N6 • 01 22 122 • www.theringhotel.com • €€€€€*

6 Hotel Regina

The Hotel Regina has a terrific view of the neo-Gothic Votivkirche – the rooms overlook the church's roof and its high stone towers. Besides a popular hotel café, the stylish Roth restaurant can be found on the ground floor. *Rooseveltplatz 15 • Map C3 • 01 404 460 • www.kremslehnerhotels.at • Dis. access • No air conditioning • €€€€*

7 Austria Trend Hotel Favorita

Built in the Art Nouveau style, this hotel has a lovely façade with red-and-gold ornamentation. As well as a ballroom with an Art Nouveau ceiling, there is a sauna, café and restaurant. *Laxenburgerstrasse 8–10 • U-Bahn U1 • 01 601 460 • www.austria-trend.at/favorita • Dis. access • No air conditioning • €€€*

8 Hilton Vienna Danube

This hotel on the banks of the Danube has its own "Active Club" with tennis, cycling and golfing. A free shuttle service goes to the centre. *Handelskai 269 • Train Handelskai; U-Bahn U6 • 01 727 770 • www.hilton.at/wiendanube • Dis. access • €€€€€*

9 Hotel Am Stephansplatz

Located in the heart of Vienna, this hotel has first-class amenities. Many rooms have a view of the cathedral. *Stephansplatz 9 • Map N3 • 01 534 050 • www.hotelamstephansplatz.at • Dis. access • €€€€€*

10 Seminarhotel Springer Schlössl

Housed in a castle built in 1887 and set in a large park, this hotel has good facilities for business travellers. *Tivoligasse 73 • Bus 9A • 01 814 2049 • www.springer-schloessl.at • Dis. access • €€*

Left **Parkhotel Schönbrunn** Right **Hotel Mailbergerhof**

TOP 10 Historic Hotels

1 Hotel König von Ungarn

As early as 1815 the "King of Hungary" hotel was established in this historic building that dates back to the 1600s. During the Austro-Hungarian monarchy, Hungarian aristocrats rented apartments here all year round. Many of their names are inscribed in the guest book. ✆ *Schulerstrasse 10 • Map N3 • 01 515 840 • www.kvu.at • Dis. access • €€€€*

2 Ambassador

Baroque architect Johann Bernhard Fischer von Erlach constructed this house in the late 17th century and in 1898 it was turned into a hotel. Famous guests have included the writer Mark Twain, actress Marlene Dietrich and composer Franz Lehár. It is still one of Vienna's most charming hotels. ✆ *Neuer Markt 5/Kärntner Strasse 22 • Map N4 • 01 961 610 • www.ambassador.at • Dis. access • €€€€€*

3 Römischer Kaiser

This hotel is housed in a Baroque palace dating from 1684 in a side street off Kärntner Strasse. The foyer and some rooms still bear historic features. ✆ *Annagasse 16 • Map N5 • 01 512 77510 • www.hotel-roemischer-kaiser.at • €€€€*

4 Parkhotel Schönbrunn

Emperor Franz Joseph I had this stately mansion built in 1907 in the elegant Hietzing district near Schönbrunn Palace to accommodate his guests. The attractive hotel offers a combination of modern amenities and imperial splendour of bygone days. ✆ *Hietzinger Hauptstrasse 10–20 • Tram 58 • 01 878 040 • www.austria-trend.at • Dis. access • No air conditioning • €€€*

5 Mercure Grand Hotel Biedermeier Wien

Housed in an early 19th-century building within walking distance of the Ring, this charming Biedermeier house has a quiet inner courtyard and a conservatory restaurant. ✆ *Landstrasser Hauptstrasse 28 • Map R4 • 01 716 710 • www.accorhotels.com • Dis. access • €€€*

6 Hotel Orient

Established in 1896, the Hotel Orient is on an old riverbank that linked the city with the Danube. It was here that trading ships unloaded cargo from the Orient. The hotel is fitted with an opulent *fin-de-siècle* interior – but note that rooms are rented by the hour. ✆ *Tiefer Graben 30–32 • Map M2 • 01 533 7207 • www.hotelorient.at • No air conditioning • €€*

7 Hotel Mailbergerhof

The history of this house dates back to the 14th century, although the original Gothic building was converted into a small Baroque palace with stables and its own chapel. The 40 rooms are cosy. ✆ *Annagasse 7 • Map N5 • 01 512 0641 • www.mailbergerhof.at • €€€*

8 Hotel Rathauspark

This hotel was the home of the Austrian writer Stefan Zweig and you can still experience the atmosphere of imperial Vienna here. It is close to the Town Hall. ✆ *Rathausstrasse 17 • Map J2 • 01 404 120 • www.austria-trend.at • Dis.access • No air conditioning • €€€€*

9 Pertschy Palais Hotel

Aristocrat Maximilian von Cavriani had a Baroque palace built here in 1734. The lovely building with an inner courtyard has rooms fitted with modern amenities. ✆ *Habsburgergasse 5 • Map M3 • 01 534 49 0 • www.pertschy.com • Dis. access • €€*

10 Wandl

This family-run hotel is in a house that dates back to 1700. It has friendly guest rooms and a large foyer. ✆ *Petersplatz 9 • Map M3 • 01 534 550 • www.hotel-wandl.com • Dis. access • No air conditioning • €€€*

***Note:** Unless otherwise stated, all hotels accept credit cards, have en-suite bathrooms and air conditioning*

Above **Hotel Austria**

Price Categories

For a standard, double room per night (with breakfast if included), taxes and extra charges.

€	under €80
€€	€80–€150
€€€	€150–€200
€€€€	€200–€280
€€€€€	over €280

Top 10 Medium-Priced Hotels

1 Hotel Austria

The Hotel Austria, located in a cul-de-sac, offers peace and quiet even though it is in the middle of Vienna. It has 42 rooms as well as four apartments, and there is also the cheaper option of picking a room without en-suite bathroom. *Fleischmarkt 20 • Map P2 • 01 515 23 • www.hotelaustria-wien.at • Dis. access • No air conditioning • €€€*

2 Am Schottenpoint

This small hotel is a friendly place with 17 rooms. It's within walking distance from the Ring and only a few minutes from the trams, buses and the underground to the centre. A breakfast buffet is included. *Währinger Strasse 22 • Map B3 • 01 310 8787 • www.schottenpoint.at • Dis. access • No air conditioning • €€*

3 Carlton Opera

Located on the edge of the centre, the Carlton Opera is an ideal starting point for exploring the city. Karlskirche is just around the corner and the Museumsquartier is nearby. The 57 rooms have tea- and coffee-making facilities. Apartments with a kitchen and family rooms are also available. *Schikanedergasse 4 • Map F3 • 01 587 5302 • www.carlton.at • Dis. access • €€*

4 Congress

This modern 3-star hotel is very close to the Belvedere. Situated just across from the former Südbahnhof on a fairly busy road, it offers good value. All 75 rooms and two apartments have satellite television as well as Internet access. *Wiedner Gürtel 34 • Map H5 • 01 505 55 06 • www.bestviennahotels.at/en/congress • Dis. access • No air conditioning • €€*

5 Cryston

The cosy and friendly rooms of the Hotel Cryston make up for its location on a busy road. The modern bedrooms are fitted with satellite TV, direct-dial phones, a safe, and hairdryers in the en-suite bathrooms. *Gaudenzdorfer Gürtel 63 • Map H1 • 01 813 5682 • www.hotel-cryston.at • No air conditioning • €€*

6 Alma Boutique-Hotel

The once modest Pension Christina has undergone a complete makeover and now has a stylish decor in shades of gold, red and brown. The hotel's 26 rooms are fitted out with modern amenities, including whirlpool baths in the luxury rooms. Located in the heart of Vienna, all the city's famous landmarks are within walking distance. *Hafnersteig 7 • Map P2 • 01 533 2961 • www.hotel-alma.com • €€€*

7 Rathaus Wine & Design

In this designer hotel close to the city centre everything revolves around wine. Each of the rooms is dedicated to a top Austrian grower, there is a wine and cheese breakfast, and wine cosmetics in the rooms. *Lange Gasse 13 • Map D2 • 01 400 1122 • www.hotel-rathaus-wien.at • Closed 22–27 Dec • €€€*

8 Schweizerhof

In the city centre, close to the Stephansdom, this family-run hotel has rooms equipped with a TV and radio. A breakfast buffet is served. *Bauernmarkt 22 • Map N3 • 01 533 19 31 • www.schweizerhof.at • No air conditioning • €€*

9 Marc Aurel

Within walking distance of the Stephansdom, this welcoming hotel has 18 rooms, some of them suitable for disabled people, and two large rooms with a kitchenette. *Marc-Aurel-Strasse 8 • Map N2 • 01 533 3640 • www.hotel-marcaurel.com • Dis. access • €€*

10 Hotel Prinz Eugen

This hotel is situated in the embassy district, close to the Belvedere. Some of the rooms are traditional and some are modern. *Wiedner Gürtel 14 • Map H5 • 01 505 1741 • www.hotelprinzeugen.at • Dis. access • €€€*

Left **Kugel** Right **Nossek**

TOP 10 Budget Hotels

1 Austria Classic Hotel Bleckmann

This cosy family-run hotel is located in the Schottenring and Alsergrund quarter, where Sigmund Freud, Franz Schubert and many other famous Viennese lived. The rooms are nicely furnished and there is a breakfast buffet. *Währinger Strasse 15 • Map C3 • 01 408 08 99 • www.hotel-bleckmann.at • No air conditioning • €€*

2 Drei Kronen Wien City

Although the building is more than 100 years old, this hotel has modern, individually furnished rooms, all equipped with TV and Internet. In the morning a breakfast buffet awaits you. The hotel is located in one of the city's booming areas, with many pubs and bars nearby. *Schleifmühlgasse 25 • Map F4 • 01 587 3289 • www.hotel3kronen.at • Dis. access • No air conditioning • €€*

3 Haydn

This 3-star hotel is located on one of the main shopping streets, Mariahilfer Strasse, and has an underground station at its front door. The rooms are quiet and are equipped with a telephone, cable TV and a minibar. There are also apartments with kitchen facilities and suites. *Mariahilfer Strasse 57–9 • Map F2 • 01 587 44 140 • www.haydn-hotel.at • €€*

4 Nossek

This B&B is located in the pedestrian zone of Graben, right in the middle of the bustling city centre. Its 26 rooms are cosy and fitted with all mod cons. There is also a TV room, and families are welcome. *Graben 17 • Map M3 • 01 533 70 41 • www.pension-nossek.at • No credit cards • €€*

5 Kolping Gästehaus

Located in a small side street, most of the modern rooms here are very quiet. The wide range of rooms suits all budgets, as you can choose between various sizes and standards. There is a breakfast buffet. *Stiegengasse 12/ Ecke Gumpendorfer Strasse • Map F3 • 01 587 5631 0 • www.kolping-wien-zentral.at • No air conditioning • €*

6 Vienna Westend City Hostel

This hostel is close to the Westbahnhof railway station and has simple rooms at reasonable rates. The building has a spiral staircase but there is also an elevator and a small garden. Facilities include a bike-locker room and a communal TV room. Rooms of various sizes are available at a broad range of rates. *Fügergasse 3 • U-Bahn U3, U6 • 01 597 67 290 • www.westendhostel.at • No air conditioning • No credit cards • €*

7 Ani

Pension Ani is a simple B&B in an old building with rooms in various sizes. It's close to the underground U6 and trams. *Kinderspitalgasse 1 • U-Bahn U6 • 01 405 65 53 • www.freerooms.at • No air conditioning • €*

8 Franzenshof

This hotel is located in the 2nd district beyond the Danube canal, close to Prater park. For smaller budgets, book a small room with shared bathroom facilities. *Grosse Stadtgutgasse 19 • U-Bahn U1 • 01 216 62 82 • www.hotel-franzenshof.at • No air conditioning • No credit cards • €*

9 Kugel

Hotel Kugel, located next to the Spittelberg area, has been in operation since 1899. It offers a relaxed atmosphere and tasteful rooms, some with four-poster beds. *Siebensterngasse 43 • Map E2 • 01 523 33 55 • www.hotelkugel.at • Closed 9 Jan–29 Feb • No air conditioning • Free Wi-Fi • €€*

10 Zur Wiener Staatsoper

Rooms of various sizes and a breakfast buffet are offered at this family-run hotel in a top location in the heart of Vienna. *Krugerstrasse 11 • Map N5 • 01 513 1274 • www.zurwienerstaatsoper.at • No air conditioning • €€*

***Note:** Unless otherwise stated, all hotels accept credit cards, have en-suite bathrooms and air conditioning*

Above **Mercure Josefshof Wien**

Price Categories

For a standard, double room per night (with breakfast if included), taxes and extra charges.

€	under €80
€€	€80–€150
€€€	€150–€200
€€€€	€200–€280
€€€€€	over €280

Top 10 Family-Friendly Hotels

1 Hotel Capri
This family-run hotel offers spacious rooms for up to four people, making them ideal for families. Located close to Prater park, there are many attractions and sports facilities nearby, and St Stephen's Cathedral is two U-Bahn stops away. *Praterstrasse 44–6 • Map R1 • 01 214 8404 • www.hotelcapri.at • No air conditioning • €€€*

2 Hotel am Parkring
Located on the Ringstrasse, this 58-room hotel offers a splendid view of the tree-lined avenue from the 13th floor. For its younger guests, books and toys are available and babysitters can be easily organized. The restaurant also provides children's menus. *Parkring 12 • Map Q4 • 01 514 800 • www.schick-hotels.com • Dis. access • €€€*

3 Hotel Stefanie
Named after the wife of Crown Prince Rudolf, Hotel Stefanie is located just beyond the Danube canal and only a few minutes' walk from the city centre. Toys and special children's menus are available, as well as reliable babysitting services. Of the 131 rooms, some include extra-large family accommodation. *Taborstrasse 12 • Map Q1 • 01 211 500 • www.schick-hotels.com • Dis. access • €€€*

4 Hotel City Central
Located on the edge of the city centre, this is an ideal point from which to discover the city. This 4-star hotel was built at the beginning of the 20th century. Children under six years stay free; children aged six to twelve stay for half-price. *Taborstrasse 8 • Map Q1 • 01 211 050 • www.schick-hotels.com • Dis. access • €€€*

5 Hotel Lassalle
This modern hotel is ideally situated for families, as the Danube island with all its lawns and cycling paths is very close by. There are family rooms and the hotel also has a games room and playroom for children with toys and books. Babysitters are arranged on request at reception. *Engerthstrasse 173–5 • U-Bahn U1 • 01 213 150 • www.austria-trend.at • Dis. access • No air conditioning • €€€*

6 Novotel Wien West
On the edge of Vienna Woods, the setting of this hotel is ideal for families. Facilities here include landscaped gardens, playgrounds, a volleyball court, table tennis and a children's menu. Babysitters are available. *Am Auhof • U-Bahn U4 • 01 979 25 420 • www.novotel.com • Dis. access • No air conditioning • €€€*

7 Mercure Josefshof Wien
Breakfast is served until noon at this hotel on a quiet road in a central location. One child under the age of 16 can stay free of charge in the parents' room. *Josefsgasse 4–6 • Map D2 • 01 404 190 • www.josefshof.com • Dis. access • €€€*

8 Hotel Anatol
Around the corner from Mariahilfer Strasse, Anatol has large family rooms. Toys are available and a babysitter can be arranged. *Webgasse 26 • Map G1 • 01 599 960 • www.austria-trend.at/hotel-anatol • Dis. access • No air conditioning • €€*

9 Harmonie-Best Western
This hotel has simple but comfortable rooms. Children under 12 years stay free. The staff will be pleased to give sightseeing tips. *Harmoniegasse 5–7 • Map B3 • 01 317 66 04 • www.bestwestern-ce.com/harmonie • No air conditioning • €€€*

10 Starlight Suite Hotel Wien am Heumarkt
With three central locations in Vienna, these spacious all-suites hotels are convenient for most sights. Kids up to age 11 stay free. *Am Heumarkt 15 • Map E6 • 01 710 78 08 • www.starlighthotels.com • Dis. access • €€€*

General Index

Acknowledgments

Main Contributors
British-born journalist and broadcaster Michael Leidig has been the *Daily Telegraph* and *Sunday Telegraph* Vienna correspondent since 1995, as well as the editor of the English-language newspaper the *Vienna Reporter* and presenter of the Austrian Broadcasting Corporation's English News service. He has lived in Austria since 1993.

Austrian journalist and broadcaster Irene Zoech has been *The Times* correspondent in Vienna since 1999, as well as Arts and Culture Editor for the English-language newspaper *Austria Today* since 1995. She is also News Editor at the press agency Central European News.

Produced by Sargasso Media Ltd, London.

Editorial Director Zoë Ross
Art Editor Clare Thorpe
Picture Research Monica Allende
Proofreader Stewart J Wild
Indexer Hilary Bird
Editorial Assistance Mariella Rihl

Main Photographer Peter Wilson
Additional Photography DK Studio/Steve Gorton, Poppy, Steve Shott, Clive Streeter

Illustrator chrisorr.com

FOR DORLING KINDERSLEY
Publishing Managers Ian Midson, Helen Townsend
Publisher Douglas Amrine
Senior Cartographic Editor Casper Morris
DTP Jason Little
Production Melanie Dowland
Picture Librarians Hayley Smith, David Saldanha
Picture Research Rhiannon Furbear
Revisions Team Louise Abbott, Namrata Adhwaryu, Lydia Baillie, Sonal Bhatt, Helen Harrison, Kaberi Hazarika, Sumita Khatwani, Shikha Kulkarni, Jude Ledger, Carly Madden, Sam Merrell, Melanie Nicholson-Hartzell, Catherine Palmi, Khushboo Priya, Quadrum Solutions, Rada Radojicic, Preeti Singh, Sadie Smith, Leah Tether, Julie Thompson, Nikky Twyman

Maps DK India: Managing Editor Aruna Ghose; Senior Cartographer Uma Bhattacharya; Cartographiwc Researcher Suresh Kumar

Picture Credits
a = above; b = below/bottom; c = centre; f = far; l = left; r = right; t = top.

The publishers would like to thank the following individuals, companies and picture libraries for their kind permission to reproduce their photographs:
AKG: Jerome da Cunha 12t, *Virgin and Child with Pear* by Albrecht Dürer 6cl, 19t, 14tl, 14tr, 14b, 16tl, 16tc, 16tr, *Peasant Wedding* by Brueghel the Elder 18b, *The Fur* by Rubens 18cr, *St George with the Scribes* 19c, *Summer* by Arcimboldo 19b, *Vienna* by Canaletto 20tl, *Portrait of Gonella* 20b, 23b, *The Chef* by Monet 24tr, *Laughing Self-Portrait* by Richard Gerstl 24b, *The Kiss* by Klimt 25b, 29b, 36–7, 37t, *Portrait of Maria Theresa* by Martin van Meytens 39b, 40tl, 40tr, *Self*

Portrait Francesco Mazzola 45, *Portrait of Beethoven* by Willibrord 58tl, *Portrait of Strauss* by August Eisenmenger 58tr, *Portrait of Mozart* by Krafft 58b, *Portrait of Mahler* by Anton Wagner-Henning 59bl, 59r; ALAMY IMAGES: Hackenberg-Photo-Cologne 78tr, 78cl.

BRIDGEMAN ART LIBRARY: Ali Meyer *Portrait of Emperor Franz Joseph of Austria 1850* by C. Lemmermayer 15b; BundesmobilienWsammlung *Elizabeth of Bavaria* by Franz Xavier Winterhalter 15t, *Crown Prince Rudolf* by Austrian School 17t; Schloss Schönbrunn *Cavalcade in the Winter Riding School* by Martin II Mytens or Meytens 17b; Kunsthistorisches Museum *Adam and Eve in the Garden of Eden* by Lukas Cranach the Elder 21t, 20tr; © DACS London 2006 Österreichische Galerie *Still Life with a Slaughtered Lamb* by Oskar Kokoschka 24tc; Centre Historique des Archives Nationales 40c; British Library 40b; Schloss Schönbrunn *Emperor Franz Joseph I of Austria* by Franz von Matsch 41t; Musée d'Art Thomas Henry *Portrait of Ferdinand I* by Frans II Pourbus 41r

CORBIS:1, Paul Almasy 88–9, Jose F. Poblete 92tl, 92tr, 130–31

DREAMSTIME.COM: Photoblueice 65tl

HOTEL KUGEL: 146tl

KUNSTHISTORISCHES MUSEUM, Vienna: 16b, 21b

ÖSTERREICHISCHE GALERIE BELVEDERE, Vienna: 6b, 22b, 22–3

PAN E WIEN: 121tl; PALAIS COBURG: Franz Zwickl 78tl

SCHÖNBRUNN KULTUR-UND BETRIEBSGES.M.B.H., Vienna: Alexander Koller 36b, Gerhard Trumler 37cr, 37b

THEATERCAFE WIEN: 115tl; THIRD MAN MUSEUM: 47tr

VIENNASLIDE, Vienna: 33ca, 62c, 62tl, 63t, 80tl, 80tr, 81t, 81r

WIEN-TOURISMUS: 33t, Janos Kalmar 96tl, Dagmar Landova 62tr

ZOOM KINDERMUSEUM: Alexandra Eizinger 29cr

All other images © Dorling Kindersley. For further information see: **www.dkimages.com**

Phrase Book

In an Emergency

Where is the telephone?	Wo ist das Telefon?	voh ist duss tel-e-fone?
Help!	Hilfe!	**hilf**-uh
Please call a doctor	Bitte rufen Sie einen Arzt	**bitt**-uh **roof**'n zee ine-en artst
Please call the police	Bitte rufen Sie die Polizei	**bitt**-uh **roof**'n zee dee poli-**tsy**
Please call the fire brigade	Bitte rufen Sie die Feuerwehr	**bitt-**uh roof'n zee dee **foyer**-vayr
Stop!	Halt!	**hult**

Communication Essentials

Yes	Ja	**yah**
No	Nein	**nine**
Please	Bitte	**bitt**-uh
Thank you	Danke	dunk-uh
Excuse me	Verzeihung	fair-**tsy**-hoong
Hello (good day)	Guten Tag	**goot**-en tahk
Goodbye	Auf Wiedersehen	owf-**veed**-er-zay-ern
Good evening	Guten Abend	goot'n **ahb**'nt
Good night	Gute Nacht	goot-uh **nukht**
Why?	Warum?	var-**room**
Where?	Wo?	**voh**
When?	Wann?	**vunn**
today	heute	**hoyt**-uh
tomorrow	morgen	**morg**'n
month	Monat	**mohn**-aht
night	Nacht	**nukht**
afternoon	Nachmittag	**nahkh**-mit-tahk
morning	Morgen	**morg**'n
year	Jahr	**yar**
there	dort	**dort**
here	hier	**hear**
week	Woche	**vokh**-uh
yesterday	gestern	**gest**'n
evening	Abend	**ah**b'nt

Useful Phrases

How are you?	Wie geht's?	vee gayts
Fine, thanks	Danke, es geht mir gut	dunk-uh, es gayt meer goot
Where is/are?	Wo ist/sind...?	voh ist/sind
How far is it to...?	Wie weit ist es...?	vee **vite** ist ess
Do you speak English?	Sprechen Sie Englisch?	shpresh'n zee **eng**-glish
I don't understand	Ich verstehe nicht	ish fair-**shtay**-uh nisht
Could you speak more slowly?	Knönten Sie langsamer sprechen?	**kurnt**-en zee **lung**-zam-er **shpresh**'n

Useful Words

large	gross	**grohss**
small	klein	**kline**
hot	heiss	**hyce**
cold	kalt	**kult**
good	gut	**goot**
bad	böse/schlecht	**burss**-uh/**shlesht**
open	geöffnet	g'**urff**-nett
closed	geschlossen	g'**shloss**'n
left	links	**links**
right	rechts	**reshts**

Making a Telephone Call

I would like to make a phone call	Ich möchte telefonieren	ish mer-shtuh tel-e-fon-**eer**'n
I'll try again later	Ich versuche noch ein mal später	ish fair-zookh-uh r nokh ine-mull **shpay**-te
Can I leave a message?	Kann ich eine Nachricht hinterlassen?	kan ish **ine**-uh nakh-risht hint-er-**lahss**-en
telephone card	Telefonkarte	tel-e-**fohn**-kart-uh
mobile	Handi	han-dee
engaged (busy)	besetzt	b'zetst
wrong number	Falsche Verbindung	falsh-uh fair-**bin**-doong

Sightseeing

entrance ticket	Eintrittskarte	ine-tritz-**kart**-uh
cemetery	Friedhof	**freed**-hofe
train station	Bahnhof	**barn**-hofe
gallery	Galerie	**gall**-er-ree
information	Auskunft	**owss**-koonft
church	Kirche	**keersh**-uh
garden	Garten	**gart**'n
palace/castle	Palast/Schloss	pallast/shloss
place (square)	Platz	**plats**
bus stop	Haltestelle	**hal**-te-shtel-uh
national holiday	Nationalfeiertag	nats-yon-**ahl**-fire-tahk
theatre	Theater	tay-**aht**-er
free admission	Eintritt frei	ine-tritt fry

Shopping

Do you have...?	Gibt es...?	geept ess
How much does it cost?	Was kostet das?	voss **kost**'t duss?
When do you open/ close?	Wann öffnen Sie? schliessen Sie?	vunn **off'n** zee **shlees**'n zee
this	das	duss
expensive	teuer	**toy**-er
cheap	preiswert	**price**-vurt
size	Grösse	**gruhs**-uh
number	Nummer	**noom**-er
colour	Farbe	**farb**-uh
brown	braun	brown
black	schwarz	**shvarts**
red	rot	**roht**
blue	blau	**blau**
green	grün	**groon**
yellow	gelb	**gelp**

Types of Shop

antiques shop	Antiquariat	antik-**var**-yat
chemist (pharmacy)	Apotheke/ Drogerie	appo-**tay**-kuh/ droog-er-**ree**
bank	Bank	**bunk**
market	Markt	**markt**
travel agency	Reisebüro	**rye-z**er-boo-roe
department store	Warenhaus	**vahr**'n-hows
hairdresser	Friseur	freezz-**er**
newspaper kiosk	Zeitungskiosk	tsytoongs-kee-osk
bookshop	Buchhandlung	**bookh**-hant-loong
bakery	Bäckerei	beck-er-**eye**
post office	Post	posst
shop/store	Geschäft/Laden	gush-**eft**/**lard**'n
shoe shop	Schuhladen	shoo-lard'n
clothes shop	Kleiderladen, Boutique	klyder-lard'n boo-**teek**-uh
food shop	Lebensmittel-geschfäft	**lay**-bens-mittel-gush-eft

Staying in a Hotel

Do you have any vacancies?	Haben Sie noch Zimmer frei?	harb'n zee nokh **tsimm**-er-fry
with twin beds?	mit zwei Betten?	mitt tsvy bett'n
with a double bed?	mit einem Doppelbett?	mitt ine'm **dopp**'l-bet
with a bath?	mit Bad?	mitt **bart**
with a shower?	mit Dusche?	mitt **doosh**-uh

I have a reservation	Ich habe eine Reservierung	ish **harb**-uh ine-uh rez-er-**veer**-oong
key	Schlüssel	shlooss'l
porter	Pförtner	**pfert**-ner

Eating Out

Do you have a table for...?	Haben Sie einen Tisch für...?	harb'n zee **ine**-uhn tish foor
I would like to reserve a table	Ich möchte eine Reservierung machen	ish **mer**-shtuh ine-uh rezer-**veer**-oong makh'n
Waiter!	Herr Ober!	hair **oh**-bare!
The bill (check)	Die Rechnung	dee **resh**-noong
breakfast	Frühstück	**froo**-shtock
lunch	Mittagessen	**mit**-targ-ess'n
dinner	Abendessen	**arb**'nt-ess'n
bottle	Flasche	**flush**-uh
dish of the day	Tagesgericht	**tahg**-es-gur-isht
main dish	Hauptgericht	**howpt**-gur-isht
dessert	Nachtisch	**nahkh**-tish
cup	Tasse	**tass**-uh
wine list	Weinkarte	vine-kart-uh
glass	Glas	**glars**
spoon	Löffel	**lerff'l**
tip	Trinkgeld	**trink**-gelt
knife	Messer	**mess**-er
starter (appetizer)	Vorspeise	**for**-shpize-uh
plate	Teller	**tell**-er
fork	Gabel	**gahb**'l

Menu Decoder

Apfel	**upf**'l	apple
Apfelsine	**upf**'l-seen-uh	orange
Aprikose	upri-**kaw**z-uh	apricot
Artischocke	arti-**shokh**-uh-	artichoke
Banane	bar-**nar**n-uh	banana
Beefsteack	**beef**-stayk	steak
Bier	beer	beer
Branntwein	brant-vine	spirits
Bratkartoffeln	brat-kar-toff'ln	fried potatoes
Bratwurst	brat-voorst	fried sausage
Brötchen	bret-tchen	bread roll
Brot	brot	bread
Brühe	bruh-uh	broth
Butter	**boot**-ter	butter
Champignon	**shum**-pin-yong	mushroom
Ei	**eye**	egg
Eis	**ice**	ice/ice cream
Ente	**ent**-uh	duck
Erdbeeren	ayrt-**beer**'n	strawberries
Fisch	**fish**	fish
Forelle	for-**ell**-uh	trout
Frikadelle	Frika-dayl-uh	hamburger
Gans	ganns	goose
Garnele	**gar**-nayl-uh	prawn/shrimp
gebraten	g'**braat**'n	fried
gegrillt	g'**grilt**	grilled
gekocht	g'**kokh**t	boiled
geräuchert	g'**rowk**-ert	smoked
Gemüse	g'**mooz**-uh	vegetables
Gurke	**goork**-uh	gherkin
Hähnchen	haynsh'n	chicken
Himbeeren	him-beer'n	raspberries
Kaffee	kaf-**fay**	coffee
Kalbfleisch	kalp-flysh	veal
Karpfen	**karpf**'n	carp
Käse	**kayz**-uh	cheese
Knoblauch	**k'nob**-lowkh	garlic
Knödel	**k'nerd**'l	noodle
Kohl	**koal**	cabbage
Kopfsalat	**kopf**-zal-aat	lettuce
Kuchen	**kookh**'n	cake
Leber	**lay**-ber	liver
Marmelade	marmer-**lard**-uh	marmalade, jam
Milch	**milsh**	milk
Mineralwasser	minn-er-**arl**-vuss-er	mineral water
Möhre	**mer**-uh	carrot
Öl	**erl**	oil
Pfeffer	**pfeff**-er	pepper
Pfirsich	**pfir**-zish	peach
Pflaumen	**pflow**-men	plum
Pommes frites	pomm-**fritt**	chips/French fries
Rindfleisch	**rint**-flysh	beef
Rotkohl	roht-koal	red cabbage
Saft	**zuft**	juice
Salat	zal-aat	salad
Salz	**zults**	salt
Salzkartoffeln	zults-kar-toff'l	boiled potatoes
Sauerkirschen	zow-er-**keersh**'n	cherries
Sekt	**zekt**	sparkling wine
Senf	**zenf**	mustard
scharf	sharf	spicy
Schlagsahne	shlahgg-zarn-uh	whipped cream
Schnitzel	**shnitz**'l	veal/pork cutlet
Schweinefleisch	**shvine**-flysh	pork
Spargel	**shparg**'l	asparagus
Spinat	shpin-art	spinach
Tee	**tay**	tea
Tomate	tom-art-uh	tomato
Wein	**vine**	wine
Wiener Würstchen	**veen**-er voorst-sh'n	frankfurter
Zitrone	tsi-trohn-uh	lemon
Zucker	**tsook**-er	sugar
Zwiebel	**tsveeb**'l	onion

Numbers

0	null	**nool**
1	eins	**eye'ns**
2	zwei	**tsvy**
3	drei	**dry**
4	vier	**feer**
5	fünf	**foonf**
6	sechs	**zex**
7	sieben	**zeeb**'n
8	acht	**uhkht**
9	neun	**noyn**
10	zehn	**tsayn**
11	elf	**elf**
12	zwölf	**tserlf**
13	dreizehn	**dry**-tsayn
14	vierzehn	**feer**-tsayn
15	fünfzehn	**foonf**-tsayn
16	sechzehn	**zex**-tsayn
17	siebzehn	**zeep**-tsayn
18	achtzehn	**uhkht**-tsayn
19	neunzehn	**noyn**-tsayn
20	zwanzig	**tsvunn**-tsig
21	einundzwanzig	**ine**-oont-tsvunn-tsig
30	dreissig	**dry**-sig
40	vierzig	**feer**-sig
50	fünfzig	**foonf**-tsig
60	sechzig	**zex**-tsig
70	siebzig	**zeep**-tsig
80	achtzig	**uhkht**-tsig
90	neunzig	**noyn**-tsig
100	hundert	**hoond**'t
1000	tausend	**towz**'nt
1,000,000	eine Million	**ine**-uh **mill**-yon

Time

one minute	eine Minute	**ine**-uh min-**oot**-uh
one hour	eine Stunde	**ine**-uh **shtoond**-uh
Monday	Montag	**mohn**-targ
Tuesday	Dienstag	**deen**s-targ
Wednesday	Mittwoch	**mitt**-vokh
Thursday	Donnerstag	**donn**-ers-targ
Friday	Freitag	**fry**-targ
Saturday	Samstag	**zum**s-targ
Sunday	Sonntag	**zon**-targ

Selected Street Index